GENERATOR™/FLASH™
WEB DEVELOPMENT

RICHARD ALVAREZ

JASON TAYLOR

MATTHEW GROCH

New
Riders

201 West 103rd Street, Indianapolis Indiana 46290

Generator/Flash Web Development

Copyright © 2001 by New Riders Publishing

International Standard Book Number: 0-7357-1080-5

Library of Congress Catalog Card Number: 00-109740

Printed in the United States of America

First Printing: April 2001

05 04 03 02 01   7 6 5 4 3 2 1

Interpretation of the printing code: The rightmost double-digit number is the year of the book's printing; the rightmost single-digit number is the number of the book's printing. For example, the printing code 01-1 shows that the first printing of the book occurred in 2001.

Warning and Disclaimer

Publisher
David Dwyer

Associate Publisher
Al Valvano

Executive Editor
Steve Weiss

Product Marketing Manager
Kathy Malmloff

Managing Editor
Sarah Kearns

Acquisitions Editor
Theresa Gheen

Development Editor
Joell Smith

Project Editor
Michael Thurston

Copy Editor
Keith Cline

Technical Editor
Mark Aiman

Cover Designer
Michael Pew

Compositor
Ron Wise

Proofreader
Debra Neel

Indexer
Lisa Stumpf

Software Development Specialist
Jay Payne

Trademarks

All terms mentioned in this book that are known to be trademarks or service marks have been appropriately capitalized. New Riders Publishing cannot attest to the accuracy of this information. Use of a term in this book should not be regarded as affecting the validity of any trademark or service mark.

Contents at a Glance

Introduction: What's the Big Deal with Site Development?   1

1   Planning Production Before Production   17

2   Designing Beyond Look and Feel   29

3   Developing the Database   47

4   Building the Templates   81

5   The Data-Entry Tool   123

6   Final Production: Putting All the Pieces Together   157

7   Conclusion   177

Appendix A: ActionScript for the Employee Navigation
Main Screen   193

Appendix B: Resources   195

Appendix C: What's on the CD-ROM   203

Table of Contents

Introduction: What's the Big Deal with Site Development?   1

Three Cheers for Macromedia Generator, Flash, and Offline
Generator Site Development   2

Assumptions   3

Development Profiles   4

Dynamic Site Development   4

Dynamic Site Development with Macromedia Generator   7

Two Flavors of Generator   7

Online Development Versus Offline Development   8

Online Generator Mode   8

Offline Generator Mode   9

The Benefits of Offline Generator Development   11

Introduction Summary   15

1 Planning Production Before Production   17

Setting the Stage for the Mock Site   17

The Workflow Process   20

Step 1: Brainstorming   21

Brainstorming Goals   21

Audience   22

Elements   22

Flow   23

Staying in Scope   24

The Final List of Sections   25

Chapter Summary   26

2 Designing Beyond Look and Feel   29

Storyboards   30

Step 2: Storyboarding the Site   31

The Goals of Site Design   39

Choreographing Movement and Pace   39

Dynamic Versus Static Design   43

Chapter Summary   45

3   Developing the Database   **47**

Introduction   47

Databases 101: Tables, Records, and Fields (Oh My!)   48

Generator/Flash 5 Data Sources   49

Databases   52

Database RAD Tools   53

Server-Side Scripting   55

The Future: XML   59

Organizing Data   61

Relationships   63

Step 3: Building the Database   65

Sample Employee Database   66

Accessing the Data (SQL 101)   75

Summary   79

4   Building the Templates   **81**

Templates and the Overall Design   82

Dynamic Elements Versus Static Elements   83

Standards and Practices   85

Edit in Place   85

Scenes   86

Layers   89

Instance-Naming Conventions   96

duplicateMovieClip (the Main Navigation)   97

with This or That   101

loadMovie   102

Image and Sound Optimization   105

The Photoshop Example   105

Generator Output   106

Library Organization   109

Working with Generator Objects   110

Step 4: Designing the Template   115
   The Goals of the Templates   115
   Incorporating Dynamic Content   115
   Library Organization Revisited   121
Cleaning House: Ridding the Template of All the Extras   122
Chapter Summary   122

5 The Data-Entry Tool   **123**
Organizing Data   124
   Clean Data Entry   125
   Example 1: Clear Placement and Realistic Data Entry 125
   Example 2: Flash Effect   127
Identifying Elements of the Data-Entry Tool   128
   The Main Navigation Page   128
   The Employee Default Page   128
   The Skills and Samples Page   130
   The Professional Biography, Personal Biography, and In
     Their Own Words Pages   132
Server-Side Scripting: ASP   134
The Goals of the Data-Entry Tool   136
Step 5: Creating a Data-Entry Tool   136
   The Main Welcome Page   137
   Modify-Content Page   143
   Update Page   146
Content-Entry Fields   148
   Text Input   148
   Image Input   148
   Input Choices   150
Previewing Content   151
Planning for Final Generator Production   155
Chapter Summary   156

6   Final Production: Putting All the Pieces Together   157

Generating Flash Movies   158

The Goals of the Final Production   158

Step 6: Generating the Site   159

Processing Templates with Generator   161

Command-Line Publishing   162

Server-Scripted Publishing   164

Supporting HTML   170

Test, Test, and Test Again   172

Deploying the Site   174

Timed Updates   174

Chapter Summary   175

7   Conclusion   177

Review: The Workflow Process   178

Step 1: Brainstorming   179

Step 2: Storyboarding the Site   180

Step 3: Building the Database   181

Step 4: Designing the Template   183

Step 5: Creating a Data-Entry Tool   184

Step 6: Generating the Site   185

Building on What We Have Built   186

Online Generator   187

New Ways to Communicate   188

Chapter Summary   191

Appendix A: ActionScript for the Employee Navigation Main Screen 193

Navigation Duplication ActionScript 193

The Control Movieclip for Scrolling 193

The Button Actions 194

Appendix B: Resources 195

Favorite Sites and Resources on the Web 195

Macromedia 195

Development and Design Resources on the Web 195

Dynamic Site Development Resources on the Web 197

Other Favorites on the Web 198

Favorite Resources on the Bookshelf 198

Software and Vendor Information 200

Appendix C: What's on the CD-ROM 203

System Requirements 203

Loading the CD Files 204

Exercise Files 204

Breakdown of Source Files by Chapter 205

Third-Party Programs 206

Read This Before Opening the Software 209

The Generator/Flash Web Development Web Site 211

Index 213

About the Authors

Richard Alvarez

Richard Alvarez and Jamie Gannon formed SurpriseMedia in September 2000, based in Chicago, IL. At SurpriseMedia, Richard serves as a technologist and evangelist for design and aesthetic development through new media. His background in writing, multimedia, Web development, and teaching are equally served in the projects at SurpriseMedia. Prior to founding SurpriseMedia, Richard was the senior Web developer for Britannica.com. Richard has been involved in all phases of new media since 1991 when he began his new media career as an intern with the Microsoft Corporation in Redmond, Washington. Since then he has played an important role in the development of award-winning CD-ROM titles, kiosks, presentations, and Web-based projects. His impressive client list includes top companies (such as Intel, Whittman-Hart (now MarchFirst), Ameritech, IBM, Boise Cascade, Sprint, Reuters, Navistar International, and Bank One). He has contributed to the production of award-winning sites, including "The Books of Hope" (**www.britannica.com/hope/**), "Worlds Apart: Regional Roots of Conflict" (**www.britannica.com/worldsapart/**), "All About Oscar" (**www.britannica.com/oscars/**), and "2000 Summer Olympics: Reflections on Glory" (**www.britannica.com/olympics/reflections/**). Richard also offers a course on journalism and new media storytelling at Northwestern University Medill School of Journalism.

Matthew Groch

Matthew Groch is the Director of Technology for 2MC, a technology consulting firm specializing in the delivery of enterprise-class systems architecture solutions. During his tenure at 2MC, Matthew has been heavily involved in a number of Web development engagements. Most notably was the development of the Britannica.com Web site, where he assisted in leading the systems architecture design and implementation efforts.

Although technically oriented, Matthew enjoys expressing his creative energies through other outlets and is looking forward to soon pursuing his goals of fiction writing, gourmet cooking, and eventually becoming an exceptional film director.

Jason Taylor

Jason Taylor is the Art Director of the Creative Department of Leapnet in Chicago after having served as a creative technologist at Britannica.com. His realm of art and technology crosses the boundaries of art's traditional mediums. Jason first began designing and developing for the Web just as a way to display his work without the boundaries of cliquish art natives and relentless galleries. Since 1995 he has designed, developed, and contributed to more than 47 Web sites and online galleries. The HyberNation Company (**www.cozycompany.com**), Wonderfulheadhurt (**www.wonderfulheadhurt. com**), Britannica.com (**www. britannica.com**), Thundralarra (**www. britannica.com/books/thundralarra**), "The Books of Hope" (**www. britannica.com/hope/**), and "2000 Summer Olympics: Reflections on Glory" (**www.britannica.com/olympics/reflections/**) are some of his more recent projects. Bridging the gap between designer and developer, Jason understands all aspects of Internet and new media production—from initial concept, to production, to quality assurance. His main focus is to develop highly interactive, aesthetically pleasing, and technologically sound new media pieces that push the current envelope well beyond the standard. One of Jason's most current manifestations is the Interactive cooperative Farcore (**www.farcore.com**). Dominantly made up of designers, the focus on the group as a whole is to partner with other freelance designers, developers, and editors to help with specific team-oriented projects.

About the Technical Editor

Mark Aiman

Mark Aiman is the Assistant Director of Information Technology for the School of Technology at Purdue University. Mark handles all aspects of Technology requirements at the School's 11 remote locations. More information about the School of Technology can be found at **www.tech.purdue.edu**. Mark is also a Systems and Software Engineer for Dynamic Systems Engineering Group (**www.dsegonline.com**). Dynamic Systems is a single-source technology solution provider that distinguishes itself by its ability to provide customized, research-supported products and services through its strategic relationships with world-class institutions of higher learning. Mark also takes pleasure in spending time outdoors, hiking, and biking.

Dedications

Richard Alvarez

This book would never have been possible without the support, guidance, and creative challenges collectively shared by so many individuals. In my professional life, I want to extend my gratitude and appreciation to all my co-workers (present and past) for their talents, their willingness to share, and for making my trips into the office a joy. In my personal life, my sisters, Pilar, Bea, and Liz, and all my family—especially my parents who, no matter what happens, believe their son is special. But most of all, to Jenn, my beautiful wife, whose patience, artistry, and friendship have shown me that life is about sharing our talents with the world and giving of ourselves.

Matthew Groch

To my parents, who have instilled in me a desire to enthusiastically explore life and seek the truth of things, and to my brother, from whom I expect significantly more profound works than this.

Jason Taylor

My fiancée Christa Aube should know her value to me is much more than working a seventy-hour workweek. (Believe it or not!) First and foremost, I could never produce anything worthwhile without her by my side. I know it sounds co-dependant, but she is truly a beautifully miraculous person. I wouldn't have slept those two hours last year without her encouragement. My work for this book and everything else I do is for her.

Acknowledgments

Richard Alvarez

I wish to acknowledge the hard work, long hours, and creative genius of my co-authors, Jason Taylor and Matt Groch. This book would not have been possible without the intelligence and creativity of so many people at Brittanica.com and Hylotek in New York, especially Andrew Nelson, Tracy Burns, Kathy Nakamura, Kathy Creech, Tom Michael, and Janet Moredock. Long live the "Books of Hope." Of course, I owe a great deal of gratitude and respect to Brandon Cox—pure brilliance! Equally important to the publication of this book are the tremendous efforts of Jennifer Alvarez, Jamie Gannon, Mike Pew, and the entire staff at New Riders Publishing, especially Theresa Gheen, Joell Smith, and Mark Aiman. Finally, for the many blessings both joyful and sorrowful, thank you to the Lord above.

Matthew Groch

I would like to thank Richard Alvarez for asking me to participate in this project and for his patience and kudos. I would especially like to thank Soniya Shrivastav for her support and confidence in my creative pursuits, and for helping me to believe that the really big events in my life really are yet to come.

Jason Taylor

I would like to acknowledge Kozaburo Suwa for letting me absorb Japanese culture in East Tennessee, of all places, and for not punching me in the face when I started talking about work and computers. Thanks again for the "fondue, rock"! We should do it again someday. I would like to thank everyone I've had the privilege of knowing and working with in this industry. Most notably: Richard Alvarez, Brandon Cox, Mike Pew, Chris Leather, and Andrew Nelson. Whether they are designing, developing, or producing, they have inspired me beyond normal comprehension.

What would anyone do without his or her closest family? Judy Coomer (Taylor), John Coomer, Nathan Taylor, James C. Brinkley, Josephine Brinkley, Aimee Coomer, Ashley Coomer, Erin Aube, Vicki Aube, and Zoe Aube.

Last but not least: Neville Brody, David Carson, Vaughn Oliver, and Paul Rand. I know it isn't a design book, but without being able to view their work, I don't know what profession I would have chosen.

Tell Us What You Think

A Message from New Riders

As the reader of this book, you are our most important critic and commentator. We value your opinion and want to know what we're doing right, what we could do better, in what areas you'd like to see us publish, and any other words of wisdom you're willing to pass our way.

As Executive Editor at New Riders, I welcome your comments. You can fax, email, or write me directly to let me know what you did or didn't like about this book—as well as what we can do to make our books better. When you write, please be sure to include this book's title, ISBN, and author, as well as your name and phone or fax number. I will carefully review your comments and share them with the authors and editors who worked on the book.

Please note that I cannot help you with technical problems related to the topic of this book, and that due to the high volume of email I receive, I might not be able to reply to every message.

Email: **steve.weiss@newriders.com**

Mail: Steve Weiss
         Executive Editor
         New Riders Publishing
         201 West 103rd Street
         Indianapolis, IN 46290 USA

Visit Our Web Site: **www.newriders.com**

On our Web site, you'll find information about our other books, the authors we partner with, book updates and file downloads, promotions, discussion boards for online interaction with other users and with technology experts, and a calendar of trade shows and other professional events with which we'll be involved. We hope to see you around.

Email Us from Our Web Site

Go to **www.newriders.com** and click on the Contact link if you

- Have comments or questions about this book.
- Want to report errors that you have found in this book.

- Have a book proposal or are interested in writing for New Riders.

- Would like us to send you one of our author kits.

- Are an expert in a computer topic or technology and are interested in being a reviewer or technical editor.

- Want to find a distributor for our titles in your area.

- Are an educator/instructor who wants to preview New Riders books for classroom use. In the body/comments area, include your name, school, department, address, phone number, office days/hours, text currently in use, and enrollment in your department, along with your request for either desk/examination copies or additional information.

Call Us or Fax Us

You can reach us toll-free at (800) 571-5840 + 9 + 3567 (ask for New Riders). If outside the U.S., please call 1-317-581-3500 and ask for New Riders. If you prefer, you can fax us at 1-317-581-4663, Attention: New Riders.

note

Technical Support for This Book. Although we encourage entry-level users to get as much as they can out of our books, keep in mind that our books are written assuming a non-beginner level of user-knowledge of the technology. This assumption is reflected in the brevity and shorthand nature of some of the tutorials.

New Riders will continually work to create clearly written, thoroughly tested and reviewed technology books of the highest educational caliber and creative design. We value our customers more than anything—that's why we're in this business—but we cannot guarantee to each of the thousands of you who buy and use our books that we will be able to work individually with you through tutorials or content with which you may have questions. We urge readers who need help in working through exercises or other material in our books—and who need this assistance immediately—to use as many of the resources that our technology and technical communities can provide, especially the many online user groups and list servers available.

Introduction:
What's the Big Deal with
Site Development?

Data-driven sites do not have to be boring, rigid, and lifeless. Rows and rows of text organized in tables do not exactly push the limits of visual design. Thanks to Macromedia Generator and Flash 5, your production of dynamic, large-content sites can have all the depth and feeling of your hand-built one-off Flash movies.

This chapter introduces you to offline Generator and the workflow process used to build compelling content-heavy sites. In particular, this chapter covers the following topics:

- Understanding Rapid Site Development with Generator and Flash 5
- Defining Your Knowledge and Skills Before Development
- Developing Sites with Generator and Flash 5
- Understanding the Two Generator Modes
- Developing in Generator Offline-Mode Benefits
- Viewing Examples of Offline Generator Sites

Three Cheers for Macromedia Generator, Flash, and Offline Generator Site Development

Hip, hip, hooray for Macromedia Flash!

Flash has taken the Web by storm. Everyone associated with Web site production knows the impact that Macromedia Flash has made on design and interactivity on the Web. If you don't, chances are that your idea of new technology is a pocket transistor radio. No other single tool has fulfilled its promise of bringing life to the Web like Flash. Designers and developers alike can easily begin using Flash and immediately create powerful results. Unlike other Web authoring technologies, Flash is not limited by browser constraints. Flash enables you to position text and graphics exactly where you want to. It also enables you to use stylized fonts and designs that will look good on all browsers and platforms. Additional benefits—such as compact vector size, robust animations, sound capabilities, and action scripting—make Flash not only a useful graphics package, but also a powerful site development tool.

Hip, hip, hooray for Macromedia Generator!

Macromedia Generator extends the capabilities of Flash by creating dynamic Flash movies, combining text, graphics, and animations from a database. Whether in real-time, running online on your Web server, or in the offline production workflow described in this book, Generator speeds up site development by allowing for large-scale Flash design in an automated fashion. The dynamic nature of Generator enables site developers and designers to customize pages with little or no effort beyond the initial template design. And because Generator works hand in hand with Flash, you can take full advantage of all the special features that Flash boasts, including animations, graphics, sound, and action scripting.

Hip, hip, hooray for offline Generator site development!

I said, hip, hip, hooray for offline Generator site development! Hello...anyone? Hmmm, am I the only one cheering? Hey where's everyone going? What's that, you've never heard of it? Well, let me fill you in.

At Surprise Media, we have developed a work process to produce media-rich sites in an offline, dynamic production process using Macromedia Generator and Flash, Microsoft Access, and Active Server Page (ASP) scripting (although Generator works with many other databases and middleware). The final production team is typically comprised of two designers and a developer. This simple approach is due to this offline process, which enables us to create a wealth of interactive Flash-based sites that consist of a large number of pages. This streamlined process enables designers, editors (content developers), and technical developers to concentrate on the disciplines they do best. Content editors work with the text, designers perfect the look, and developers put it all together in the final site design.

This book is targeted specifically at the community of fellow developers, designers, Web producers, and project managers. The goal is to demonstrate the offline, dynamic Generator techniques to those who want to take advantage of the power of Macromedia Flash 5 and Generator templates, as well as those who are interested in rapid site development. This book focuses mainly on the workflow process, from initial creative inspiration through the production of an entire site. You will walk through every step of the offline, dynamic site development process. Rather than read about specific topics in an unrelated manner, you will deconstruct the development of an actual site from beginning to end. The goal is to present all the hot topics and techniques, as well as wrap all those ideas into a related package that brings it all together. Along the way, sample code, illustrations, and notes accompany the explanations. The ideas covered and lessons learned will give both designers and developers new tools to quickly produce large, content-heavy sites.

Assumptions

So are you ready to create? Well, first let's review some assumptions about your knowledge of site development and the tools you need to get going.

The topics covered here presume the basic knowledge of HTML and client/server-side scripting. General Flash animation and action scripting techniques should already be in your bag of tricks, as well. Likewise, the specifics of database connectivity, SQL commands, and Generator-specific coding issues are beyond the scope of this book. This book does, however, cover general topics on ASP scripting for Generator, connecting to databases, and working with data sources. The chapters that follow take advantage of these techniques in the final design of the mock site, and all along the way you see code samples and explanations that cover just enough for you to build it.

This book presents a foundation to work from and build upon and, as previously stated, introduces you to the offline Generator site development workflow. Use the concepts and ideas in this book as a springboard as you expand your knowledge of server-side scripting, SQL, and databases. The specific details about these disciplines are beyond the scope of this book. For more information about such technologies and code samples, refer to Appendix A for resources on Active Server Pages, dynamic site development, database connectivity, and Generator white papers. The appendix also contains some of our favorite sites, books, and resources on these subjects.

Development Profiles

To give you a complete picture of the workflow process, the list that follows describes the hardware and software used to build the mock site in this book. We completed all work on two machines, a PC and a Macintosh (a shining example of how the world can come together to work in perfect harmony).

PC

1. 850MHz Pentium III processor
2. 128MB RAM
3. Windows 2000 with IIS 5.0
4. Microsoft Personal Web Manager 5
5. Macromedia Generator Developer Edition
6. Macromedia Flash 5
7. Microsoft Access 2000
8. Allaire Homesite 4.0.5

> **note**
>
> **Allaire and Macromedia.** At the printing of this book, Macromedia's acquisition of Allaire was not yet finalized. The references in this book and on the accompanying CD-ROM to Homesite and ColdFusion reflect this pending acqusition.

Macintosh

1. Macintosh G4
2. OS 9
3. 196MB RAM
4. Macromedia Flash 5
5. Adobe Photoshop 5.5
6. Adobe Illustrator 8.0

For software and system requirements specified by Macromedia, refer to the appendix or visit Macromedia at **www.macromedia.com**.

Dynamic Site Development

Dynamic site development is not new. Many large corporations, such as Microsoft and IBM, use databases and both client- and server-side scripting to build and publish Web sites. This method of automated Web site development allows for daily or even hourly content to be posted easily and quickly. It also can provide customers with a personalized site experience by providing specific content that users can select from instantaneously. Popular sites such as eBay and Yahoo! use dynamic technologies to offer their customers personalized pages tailored to provide information users have previously selected or shown an interest in (see Figures I.1 and I.2).

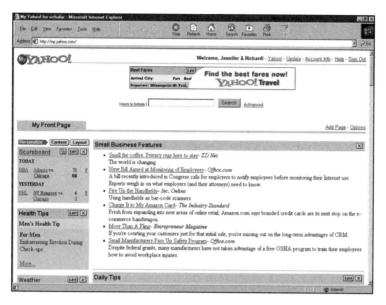

FIGURE I.1   *Sites such as Yahoo! use dynamic technologies that enable customers to personalize the look and content that appear on their sites.*

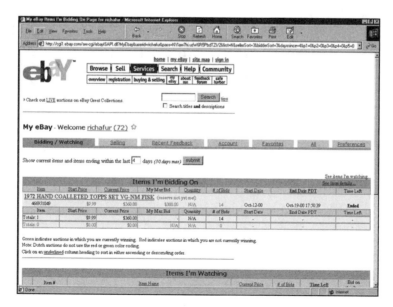

FIGURE I.2   *eBay also uses the same dynamic technologies that enable customers to personalize the look and content that appear on their sites.*

At Britannica.com, for instance, most of the content you see is published using dynamic technologies. Daily feeds from wire services and content providers, such as Reuters and *The Washington Post*, provide news and up-to-date information on various topics, including top news stories, financial reports, and the up-to-the-minute sports scores. Likewise, many in-house articles are created days, sometimes weeks in advance and posted dynamically at a later date using the same dynamic backend server technologies.

Award-winning interactive spotlights and features on Britannica.com, created with Generator and Flash, use similar dynamic technologies. Such features as "The Books of Hope: Hope for a New Millennium" (see Figure I.3), "Olympics 2000: Reflections on Glory," and "Olympics 2000: Around the World" go beyond the standard grid layout of text headings and data. Through the use of music, sound events, images, and screen transitions, audiences "experience" the site rather than just click from screen to screen. Success comes not only in presenting content (And because they are the Encyclopaedia Britannica, they have volumes of content!), but also in telling a story. Flash development alone enables you to use sound and animation to evoke an emotional response from your audience. Generator development enables you to accomplish that same level of emotional response in storytelling, but in a larger scale and with a faster turnaround.

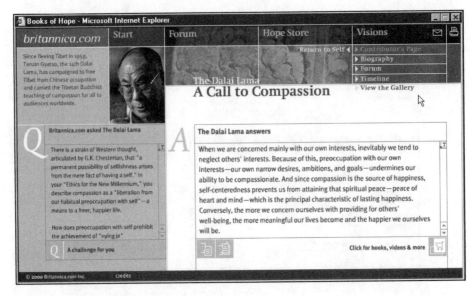

FIGURE I.3   *The Books of Hope presents a forum that invites an audience to read and discuss the hopes and beliefs of some of the worlds foremost thinkers.*

Dynamic Site Development with Macromedia Generator

Macromedia Generator is a dynamic site development solution that makes data-driven Web sites possible. Unlike other dynamic site development technologies, however, Generator takes graphical elements in addition to text as variable data. What this means is that in addition to dynamically posting the latest sports scores, you also could conceivably post the appropriate sport animation to go with it.

A cookie-cutter approach to site development separates the various tasks into a more efficient, streamlined process. By using Generator/Flash 5 technologies, designers and developers are not repeatedly creating one-off versions of the same Flash movie to accommodate variable content. Likewise, editorial staff or content creators do not have to concern themselves with the technological requirements of producing Flash movies and supporting HTML to go with it.

Two Flavors of Generator

Macromedia offers Generator in two distinct flavors: Generator 2 Enterprise Edition, and Generator 2 Developer Edition. Although both editions facilitate dynamic content publishing, they do have key differences (for instance, the amount of content being updated, how often the updates happen, and the costs involved in supporting the development).

Generator 2 Enterprise is a real-time dynamic solution for site developers who demand high-performance and time-sensitive content updates. It comes with a sophisticated caching feature that reduces the load of page updates by your server. It also helps keep your audience happier by producing quicker page views. As of this writing, the price of the Generator 2 Enterprise Edition starts at $30,000 for a site license.

Generator 2 Developer Edition is essentially the same package. However, it does not have the robust architecture that enables you to produce high-volume updates in real-time. Therefore, Macromedia promotes its Developer Edition of Generator on their Web site and in promotional literature as the solution for creating "Web proto-types for customers whose requirements may scale to include real-time and person-alized content and for low-volume sites." As of this writing, the price of Generator Developer Edition starts at $999 per server (although certain special updates enable you to buy it for less than that). Of course, the quickest and easiest way to get start-ed is to download the free Generator authoring extensions and a 30-day free trial of Generator 2 Developer Edition. You can do so at **www.macromedia.com/ soft-ware/generator/trial/**.

Online Development Versus Offline Development

In addition to the two different editions of Generator, there are also two modes of publishing with Macromedia Generator: online mode and offline mode. Each has its benefits and ideal uses. The workflow process used to build the mock site in this book uses offline Generator. Before you jump into offline development, however, it is a good idea to see what each Generator mode is all about.

Online Generator Mode

In the online mode of Macromedia Generator, the template lives on the Web server and the request to generate (or create a dynamic instance of the template as a Flash movie) is initiated by the end user hitting that particular page in the browser. (See Figure I.4.)

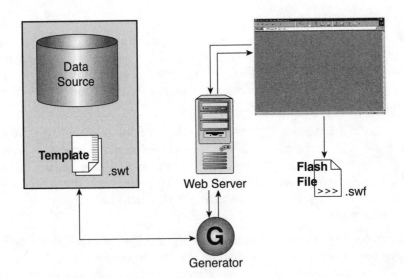

FIGURE I.4   *The Online Generator process.*

Online Generator Steps

1. The browser requests a template. (The Web server starts an instance of Generator on the server.)

2. Generator loads a template.

3. Generator reads a data source.

4. Generator merges media.

5. The server returns a Macromedia Flash movie to the browser (or animated GIF, GIF, JPEG, PNG, text file, image map, QuickTime movie, or Windows or Mac self-executing movies or projectors).

6. Repeat for every new user who visits the page.

The most important thing to consider when deciding between online and offline Generator development is the volume of dynamic requests required. Put another way, how often does the content you show on your Web site need to update? This difference essentially determines not only which mode of Generator publishing you use, but also which edition of Generator you purchase.

If you are showcasing an online store where customers can customize and view products on demand, for instance, you are most likely talking online Generator here. Suppose, however, that your site uses Flash to create an interactive banking system application, whereby customers can access their accounts, transfer funds, pay bills, and so on. You can design such a tool as a template and then populate it with specific customer data using Macromedia Generator. And yes, you guessed it, depending on the volume of hits your Web site receives, this is once again best suited for online Generator.

Beyond the technological differences, there's the cost of implementing these two different modes of Generator development. Online Generator development is an enterprise solution that dramatically affects the way a company structures their Web deployment architecture. In a nutshell, due to the cost of the Enterprise Edition of Macromedia Generator and the required hardware, software, and staff needed to deploy such online Generator sites, it is a solution that is right for only certain larger corporations and institutions.

Offline Generator Mode

In offline Generator mode, the request to generate the template into the data-specific Flash movie comes from you, the designer/developer rather than the server. In simple terms, you determine when the template gets generated. Once you do generate, what you are left with is a regular SWF Flash movie that you can post to the server just like any other Web media element (be it a GIF, JPG, PDF, or so on). (See Figure I.5.)

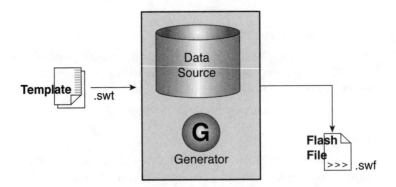

FIGURE 1.5   *The offline Generator process.*

Offline Generator Steps

1. Generator loads the template.
2. Generator reads the data source.
3. Generator merges media.
4. The application returns a file (SWF, GIF, PNG, JPEG, or QuickTime) to the server.
5. The Web server can then serve this output file as it does any other file.
6. Repeat for every new user who visits the page.

Once again, consider the volume of dynamic requests required by your server. When the content you present on your site needs to update less frequently, you are ready for offline Generator development.

Suppose your e-commerce site showcases an interactive product-of-the-week feature. You can create a template that contains a standard splash screen, pricing, product details, a fun interactive gallery, and of course, ordering information. Your inventory may contain hundreds, perhaps thousands of products. Offline Generator is a perfect solution in this case. In this example, the content of each product feature is the same for each visitor and each is generated and posted only once a week. And because the offline

Updates and Traffic. A less frequently updated site does not necessarily mean less traffic. The two are completely independent of each other. Your high-traffic site displays your Flash content as it does any other request made by the browser (HTML, images, and so on) because the server does not handle the updates or tasks of generating updated content. With offline Generator, you control when the latest content is posted to the server.

mode creates a static SWF file, you also are building an archive (or inventory) of product movies that can be referenced from the site. If any of the product movies need to be updated with new information (a change in price, for instance), offline Generator comes to the rescue again.

Macromedia now bundles Generator 2 Developer Edition and Flash 5 together. This bundling essentially puts dynamic Generator development into the hands of many who might not be able to afford to publish and experiment with the Enterprise Edition. Because offline Generator development does not run off of your Web sever, but instead as an application, the cost of supporting Generator development generates substantial savings as well. Although you can have high-end servers hosting your database, Web services, and Generator, they are not essential. You can just as easily produce the content of the mock site described in the subsequent chapters by running Microsoft Personal Web Server (offered free from Microsoft) from your local machine. See the Macromedia Generator tutorial PDF on the CD-ROM for Macromedia's server and authoring system requirements.

note

This book describes using offline Generator to create Flash content. Note, however, that some offline Generator techniques described here, with minor adjustments, are excellent ways to create dynamic JPG, GIF, animated GIF, PNG, QuickTime, image maps, and text files too.

The Benefits of Offline Generator Development

Now you should have a good idea of what Generator can do (both Enterprise and Developer Editions). In addition, you should feel comfortable discussing the use of online and offline Generator modes. If Enterprise Edition is the right solution for your site, this book is probably not the best-suited material for your needs. In an online Enterprise situation, you will most likely have a server support team, programmers, and Web managers at your service in addition to a whole library of materials relating to server-side scripting, site architecture, and databases.

On the other hand, if offline Generator will serve your content-producing needs, you have come to the right place. This book demonstrates and guides you through the offline Generator workflow process. In the end, you gain the know-how to begin creating your own dynamic Flash site using ideas and techniques from this book.

The core purpose of this book is to demonstrate the use of Macromedia Generator and Flash 5 to create outstanding design and depth in large-content site development in offline mode. When content does not need to be updated as often, offline mode Generator is a perfect solution for developing very creative, very rich, very robust sites packed with all the sound, animation, and Flash greatness your audience demands.

This book shows you how to maintain the high-end design and motion graphics your Flash movies already have, and how to use them to quickly deploy larger volume content sites. By following a workflow process that has already been successfully implemented, you will go through the entire offline Generator site development life cycle. We do not pretend to have all the answers. The methods and examples discussed here are but only one of many ways to accomplish the goals at hand. The intention is to demonstrate a proven method that is very accessible, both in the level of Web practices and cost, to the vast community of Web developers, designers, and content producers.

Many good examples of such high-end Flash content sites are being published today. The possibilities of such types of sites are endless. The following figures (I.6 - I.10) contain perfect example candidates that would work well as high-end Flash content sites using offline Generator development.

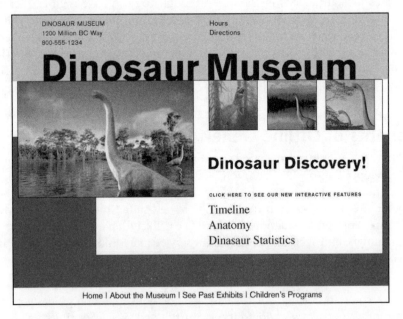

FIGURE I.6   *Museums, galleries, special libraries, and zoos can showcase their exhibits in a detailed virtual environment.*

FIGURE 1.7   *Newspapers, magazines, and journals can spotlight a template design to highlight a special person or group, place, or event.*

FIGURE 1.8   *E-commerce sites can feature a product or entire catalog.*

FIGURE 1.9   *Government, university, and information sites can show off how-to segments on a variety of subjects.*

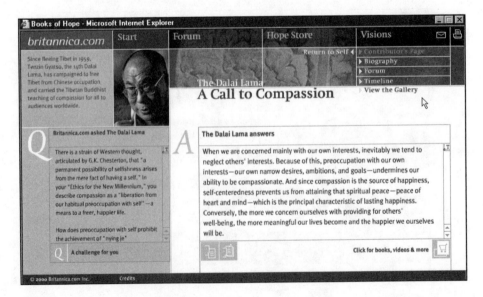

FIGURE 1.10   *Britannica.com's feature "The Books of Hope: Thoughts for a New Millennium" uses offline Generator development to share the thoughts and feelings of 16 influential contributors from around the world (**www.britannica.com/hope**).*

Introduction Summary

In this chapter, you explored the following topics:

- **Dynamic site development.** Data-driven sites give audiences up-to-date information, personal attention, and custom-tailored design.

- **Generator.** Generator is a dynamic server solution that comes in two distinct flavors: Enterprise and Developer Editions. In addition, there are two modes of generating Flash movies with Generator: online mode and offline mode.

- **Generator online mode.** Developing in Generator online mode is an enterprise solution that requires supporting hardware, software, and staff. It is best suited for sites that need personalization in real-time.

- **Generator offline mode.** Developing in Generator offline mode provides an affordable way to build Flash sites rapidly. It is best suited for sites where content is the same for all users and requires less-frequent updates. Site development in Generator offline mode offers all the benefits of one-off Flash site development, but in larger scales and with quicker delivery.

There has been a change in the old guard as far as data-driven sites are concerned. As designers, developers, and content providers, you now have greater options to add life and feeling in your content-heavy sites. Generator and Flash 5 give you the tools to quickly create high-volume content sites that are both dynamic in the way they present and update data, and also aesthetically pleasing to the senses.

This chapter introduced you to dynamic site development using Macromedia Generator and Flash 5, the two distinct Generator editions, and the two separate Generator modes. Now that you have a fundamental understanding of Macromedia Generator, you should be able to define which mode of Generator would make the most sense for your projects. This basic knowledge also gives you the foundation to begin building the mock employee site that serves as an example throughout this book. Chapter 1 introduces you to the first of six steps in the Generator offline workflow process, brainstorming.

CHAPTER 1

Planning Production Before Production

The Introduction introduced you to the Generator and offline-mode development, which you can use to build compelling content-heavy sites. In this chapter, you expand your understanding of site development by working with a mock employee site. This site gives you a chance to work with offline Generator and to learn about the workflow process. The first step in the workflow process is brainstorming to determine the site's audience, elements, and page-to-page flow.

This chapter focuses on brainstorming, the first in a six-step workflow process using offline Generator. In particular, this chapter covers the following topics:

- Setting the stage
- Introducing the offline Generator workflow process
- Brainstorming
- Determining the audience
- Determining elements
- Determining flow

Setting the Stage for the Mock Site

Okay, now that you know a little bit about dynamic site development and how to build sites with Generator and Flash 5, it is time to build a Generator/Flash 5 site.

Here's the deal: Awesome Flash development is what your client expects from you. Your company is more than an award-winning design firm. Content is what separates you from every other bells-and-whistles Flash design house. You always aim for site creation beyond Flash for Flash sake. You do not treat your client's brand as just a logo; it influences the entire site development (beyond banner ads or a single-page focus). Your sites tell stories that evoke feelings and emotions. They demand emotional responses from your audience. A message emanates from the flow and movement of your creations. The build and tempo of your animations are purposeful. That purpose also influences the choice of colors and the tempo of sounds. Put simply, it is all about content.

Here's the setting for the mock employee site. You are about to deliver the biggest proposal your firm has ever prepared. If accepted, your company will be the exclusive content providers for Big International Company. As if the pressure to deliver is not high enough already, your boss tells you, "We must get this account!" Oh, one more thing. You are scheduled to deliver in less than a month.

So how will your proposal stand above the rest? Lucky for you, here's some inside information. You have heard that the president of Big International Company likes to work with firms that she feels very comfortable with. In fact, you have heard that the managers of Big International Company customarily request interviews with all staff members of the firms it works with (in an effort to get to know them personally).

That is exactly the kind of information a brilliant person like you needs to run with. Here's the plan. Aside from the cutting-edge Flash design and development your team is famous for producing, your proposal will contain the secret winning ingredient: Your pitch to Big International Company will introduce your staff of 50 artists, developers, producers, and mangers who make up your entire team.

You will design a virtual-reality meeting room in which Big International Company can meet and learn about everyone in your firm at their own pace—a place where team members can present samples of their best work, present their professional and personal goals, and perhaps even list some of their favorite links, foods, movies, and so on. As if that would not be enough, you will go beyond the rigid database result page style. Each unique employee page will feature the cutting-edge design and motion graphics that showcase the level of talent of which you are capable. The project will exemplify the superior motion graphic design in Flash that makes your firm stand above the rest. No doubt it will have stylish typography, sophisticated transitions, and appropriate music and ambient sounds. More than anything else, however, the most important ingredient will be its content.

- Detailed information on each employee, with separate sections to present information in a clear and intuitive manner.

- Transitions to introduce the various sections and build the user interface.

- Interactive elements to navigate through the site.

- Appropriate sound elements to breathe life and mood to complete the user experience.

"Okay! That sounds wonderful," you say, "but almost every member on staff is currently booked on other projects." How and when are you supposed to get this done? Is each person responsible for creating his or her own set of pages? And if so, are you jeopardizing a consistent look for the entire site? With such a tight delivery schedule, is this even possible? You have 50 individual staff members and need a minimum of 5 pages from each; so, you require a minimum of 250 unique pages. You must manage the creation of all those separate pages and incorporate them together. And these tasks are supposed to be completed when?

You could include a Flash movie for each individual and build them one by one. Sure, and you also could make a note to get everything right the first time. Beyond the simple fact that this approach is vastly inefficient and a tedious wasteful effort, the clear reason not to do this is that change is inevitable. Also, consider the enormous room for error that such repetitive actions can create.

Do any of the following examples sound familiar?

Example 1. No sooner are you finishing up on one Flash movie, when you get a request to change the employee role from Creative Director to Creative Technologist.

Example 2. You review your finished work and find a typo in the spelling of your own name.

Example 3. The ultimate kicker. You finish all 50 unique employee movies and during the final review session learn that employee roles should be abbreviated and lowercase.

Even the smallest change requires that each individual Flash movie be reopened. There must be a better way, right?

Whoa, before you tear all your hair out, allow me to paint a perfect site development picture for you.

The Workflow Process

Suppose that you have one consistent design template. With this in place, each staff member uses the template to "generate" his or her own unique movie. Incorporating the usual set of Flash "wows," the centerpiece of the site is the data. The data is not tied to the actual Flash movies, but instead is housed outside of the Flash movie in a central database. You enable data entry via a familiar Web authoring tool. (See Figure 1.1.)

In such a workflow process, if for any reason content needs to be modified, added, or deleted, changes can be easily made and reflected on the site instantly—no more changes to one-off pages and the nightmare that comes from project managing hundreds of static Flash movies. Instead you work from a single template to dynamically generate all 50 movies. Each team member can concentrate on his or her own data, and not the actual design and development specifics. Likewise, the design/development process is separated from the content. At the heart of the workflow process are these three important basic elements:

1. Database
2. Data-entry tool
3. The template

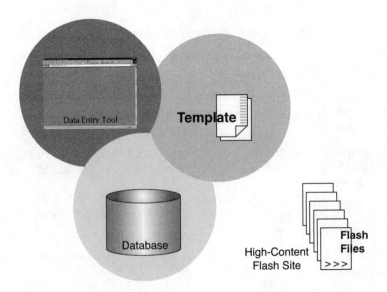

FIGURE 1.1   *The elements of the workflow process.*

Sound too good to be true? Welcome to the "offline" Generator site development workflow process. Here's the formula for building a high-end Flash site:

1. Brainstorming
2. Storyboarding the Site
3. Designing the Template
4. Building the Database
5. Creating a Data-Entry Tool
6. Generating the Site

This chapter discusses the first step in the workflow process, brainstorming. The following five chapters take an in-depth look at the remaining steps individually. Each step will help you to build the mock site that was just introduced. Although some of the steps occur simultaneously and overlap, the process always begins with planning.

Step 1: Brainstorming

The first step in the workflow process is brainstorming. What exactly are you going to do? Who are you doing this for? How will you build it? Brainstorming enables you to consider options, good and bad, and to plan for all aspects of production. Planning before production cannot be stressed enough. Nothing will kill your project faster than lack of planning. Every great site (and even the not-so-great ones) should have at least one-third of the entire project devoted to planning. If you can get away with it, even more wouldn't hurt.

It is a good idea to introduce delivery and budget estimates now, if possible. This will help keep ideas in scope. That being said, a good brainstorming meeting should still contain its share of pie-in-the-sky ideas. Although it may not be possible to complete such concepts due to time and/or budget constraints, such ideas open the doorway to more creative solutions. When you aim high and then scale back to what fits in scope (time, budget, design/development resources), the results are usually pretty good solutions that you may not have thought of otherwise. And that is the very essence of brainstorming.

Brainstorming Goals

The goal of every brainstorming meeting is to answer the following questions:

- Who is the audience?
- What elements will make up the site?
- What is the general flow of the site?

Audience

Knowing who will visit and use the employee site (or any project you're working on) will greatly help you narrow the scope of ideas that will determine the final content, look and feel, and flow of the site. With your audience in mind, you can structure a design to meet their needs and expectations. Their skill-levels, backgrounds, and goals of using your site will vary from beginners to experts. Novice users may need special instructions that walk them through the functionality and organization of information in the site. "Power users," on the flip side, may see this type of guidance as an obstacle in getting to the content. A well-designed and thought-out system should be able to accommodate a range of user skills and interests.

If you were to create a project specifically for children, for instance, your ideas might include bright colors, kid-friendly iconography, and simple and fun language. On the other hand, if the audience for your project is visiting for business purposes, your ideas might include corporate-identity colors, business charts and tables, and professional language and industry-specific lingo.

As discussed in the "Setting the Stage for the Mock Site" section, the employee site is being specifically created for the management team at Big International Company. Because the site will serve as your team's welcoming gesture to Big International Company, you know that it needs to introduce each employee in a warm and friendly manner. In addition, because the site is part of the big-pitch proposal, it needs to include a cool, clean, and simple design as well as those special "wow" features that can showcase your team's Flash design talents.

Elements

Think of the site as a dinner party. Should you prepare hors d'oeuvres only, or a seven-course meal? Are you serving soup or salad, or perhaps both? After you have answered these high-level questions, you can concentrate on preparing the individual dishes. Only then can your attention focus on the actual ingredients, or in this case color, placement, and motion (in other words, the look and feel).

So what should the dinner party or site contain? Things such as professional and personal goals, work samples, and lists of favorites were mentioned earlier. Because this is a brainstorm, you are not concerned with getting everything exactly right. Rather, you are looking for ideas to build on and problem areas to avoid. So building on the initial list, begin by naming things off the top of your head.

Site Elements

1. Information about each employee
2. Professional biography
3. Personal biography
4. Expertise and skills
5. Education
6. Links to work samples
7. Interests (hobbies, books, movies, TV shows, and so on)
8. Space for a personal message
9. Video greeting
10. Motto
11. Work slideshow
12. Awards and honors
13. Human oddity

Flow

That's a pretty good list. Except for that "human oddity" thing. You ran out of delicious Chicago-style pizza and people might have been getting a little antsy. Not to worry, because your brainstorming session has given you enough to go on. Now you can begin to organize these ideas into site flow that makes sense for your audience and to focus on the content of the site.

Including all these listed ideas would make for a very crowded and unstructured clutter of information on a single page. Instead, you should arrange the content into five distinct pages. Doing so will make content easier to display and read, and users will be able to find specific information on employees quickly (and logically). An employee default start page will contain employee information (such as birthday and hometown, the list of favorites, and, of course, a photo of each employee). You can use the default start page as a menu to the other sections.

Like the default employee start page, you are also going to need some sort of main menu page. This page will give you access to each individual employee page. Call this page the Main Navigation page. This page brings the total number of unique pages in this site to 251 pages (50 employees × 5 pages per employee + an additional Main Navigation page).

Staying in Scope

Take time to consider whether your brainstorming ideas fit within the delivery timeframe for the project. Considering this window of time, you must wisely prioritize items from the list. By doing so, you can determine not only the essential elements that have to go into the employee site, but also all those that can realistically fit into the development timeframe as well.

The proposal is due in about three weeks, give or take a few days. The job now is to narrow the scope of the site to a manageable and workable entity, keeping in mind that selecting the elements of the site is only the first step. Once selected, each element must be planned, designed, and developed. Knowing this, things such as a video greeting are great, but not realistic. Considering the time to shoot, edit, and incorporate each piece into the development of the site, the entire three weeks could be eaten up on this element alone.

Something else to consider is the fact that not everyone on staff has a formal education in design or programming. And only a handful of team members have received an award or honor. Instead of highlighting "Education" and "Awards and Honors" sections, it would be better to incorporate those elements into the "Professional" or "Personal Bio" sections. In the same way, you can combine "Expertise and Skills," "Links to Sample Works," and "Work Slideshow" sections together into a common "Skills and Samples" section.

note

Reality Check. The mock employee site contains an open budget. In reality, however, even proposals have allotted budgets. Does your firm have video-editing capabilities? Or will it have to out-source these types of components? In either case, these types of features (as do all) cost time and money. Just as important to fitting development-wise into the delivery timeframe, each element must fit into the estimated budget.

It is pointless to plan for an all-out, state-of-the-art, high-bandwidth movie experience if the delivery schedule and budget does not allow it. Although you are not concerned with the exact look, color, or placement of objects just yet, it is helpful to narrow brainstorming ideas to those that will fit in scope.

When you are trying to decide when and what to consolidate from a brainstorming list, keep in mind that what you are building is a dynamic site based on a template design. It does not make sense to build a section into the design specifically tailored for one or two employees.

Consider the mock employee site, for example. You might have a magnificent 3-D artist on staff. One brainstorming idea was to have a virtual-reality gallery to view samples and enter 3-D environments. Although there is no doubt that it would be a very cool way to present the 3-D artist's samples, it probably would not work for the other 49 team members.

Consider the dinner-party metaphor again: Better to serve a menu of courses that everyone will enjoy, instead of preparing each individual meal separately.

The Final List of Sections

Your tremendous planning efforts have determined the final list of six sections in the employee site. The final list of site elements looks like this:

1. Main Navigation

2. Employee Default Page

3. Professional Biography

4. Personal Biography

5. Skills and Samples

6. In Their Own Words

Just by listing the different pages this way, the site is already beginning to take shape. It also begins to show some of the holes. For instance, you need some way to move between the main page and the individual employee pages, and vice versa. Should you have all employee pages accessible throughout the site in the form of a main navigational element that stays onscreen at all times? Or should you move back and forth between the main menu page and employee pages? On that same note, once inside an employee page, you need to access the different sections that make up each employee page.

Again, the purpose of brainstorming is to identify the separate elements of the site, not the specific details of the design or development. The fact that you are thinking about other processes in the workflow is an added bonus. It is always important to keep the big picture in mind throughout every step of development (for example, keeping the template approach intact). If at any point you see an area that demands customization, it should raise a red flag. Such individual attention to a particular section is moving away from the purpose of creating a template and separating content from design. Note how the selected sections of the mock employee site can easily be adapted into a template design.

With the final pages determined, you can take an overall look at the site navigation (flowchart) in the template design. (See Figure 1.2.)

note

Scope Creep. Beware of scope creep. As stated earlier, brainstorming meetings are meant to introduce "pie-in-the-sky" ideas and concepts. By the end of your brainstorming sessions, however, you should determine what fits within the scope and what might be left for a subsequent version. Take the necessary time up front during the brainstorming sessions to think through all ideas and how they will fit in the scope of your project. After you have agreed on elements and flow of the site, *always move forward* to complete the project. This means that when project design and development begins, never revisit or try to brainstorm ideas again. Doing so is a sure way to blow your delivery schedule, project budget, and the patience of your entire staff.

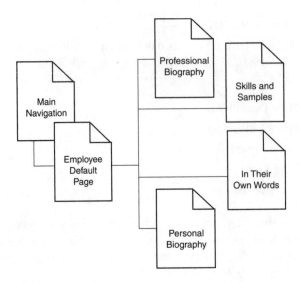

FIGURE 1.2   *The final pages arranged in a flowchart.*

In creating the final list of sites elements, the brainstorming goals are complete. The precise details of the site's look and feel are better left to expert designers and Web developers. Speaking as a developer, they will thank you for putting in this much initial planning and effort to narrow the precise scope of the site before their actual work begins.

The next step begins where brainstorming sessions leave off. Building on the current high-level design of the site, you start narrowing in on the final design by storyboarding the movement and placement of actual elements. The next chapter discusses this step. No time to take a break, the real fun is just about to begin.

Chapter Summary

In this chapter, you explored the following topics:

- **The mock employee site.** The stage is set for the rest of this book. You now have the context from which to build the mock employee site.

- **Offline Generator components.** The three main components in the offline Generator workflow process are the template, the database, and the data-entry tool.

- **The workflow process.** The six steps in the offline Generator workflow process are brainstorming, storyboarding the site, designing the template, building the database, creating a data-entering tool, and generating the site.

- **Brainstorming.** The first step in the offline Generator workflow process is brainstorming. Brainstorming enables you to identify the audience, the separate elements, and the flow of the site before design and development. During your brainstorming sessions, keep in mind delivery timetables, project budgets, and scope creep.

Planning is perhaps the most important step in any project development. Brainstorming is the first step in the planning process. It gives you the chance to explore a variety of possible directions, both in and out of scope. All options should be considered and evaluated. Even those options that are not developed are still valuable because they force you to consider what does and does not allow you to pursue them. Also, they may spark discussion in a more appropriate direction.

This chapter introduced you to the challenge of creating a data-driven employee information site. You began by determining the mock employee site's role and audience. Based on that crucial information, you got started on the first step in the workflow process: brainstorming. Your brainstorming meetings determined the elements, pages, and flow of the site. In addition, with timetables and budgets in mind, you were able to gain a better understanding of the overall site and plan for keeping the entire project within scope. With the results defined in your brainstorming sessions, you are now ready to take those ideas and put them into practice. In the next chapter, you create the storyboards that will serve as your blueprint for the construction of the employee site.

CHAPTER 2

Designing Beyond Look and Feel

This chapter discusses the planning and preparation of site design using storyboards. Working off of productive brainstorming sessions with the group, the momentum continues into the site design. When the work in this chapter is complete, you will have a complete blueprint to build and design the employee site. Every aspect from placement and spacing to navigating and transition between employee pages is covered in detail. This essential step in the workflow process enables you to lay the groundwork for building your site without looking back and redesigning for changes that might come along. More importantly, the current site will have a "guide" to show where, when, and how content is displayed.

This chapter shows how to create storyboards. It is the second step in a six-step workflow process using offline Generator, and a crucial part of site planning and development.

In particular, this chapter covers the following topics:

- Defining site design
- Understanding the use of storyboards in site design
- Building site design
- Identifying dynamic and static elements
- Planning for scalable look-and-feel design with Flash

Storyboards

With the completion of the brainstorming session from the preceding chapter, the next step in our development process is to create the plans (or storyboards) for the Flash movies. Storyboards are essential to any site development, regardless of the tools or scripting language involved in the development. Because the chosen production method in this case involves Flash, however, they play an especially important role.

Why? The Web is quickly evolving into a medium that closely resembles television and film. In those media, storyboards are essential for three reasons: To describe the scenes, to define the action, and to reveal the progression of the production. At its very heart, Flash, as an animation tool, is no different from motion pictures or television.

With regard to Flash, the goal of storyboards is to visually help everyone on your team, as well as your client, to

- Understand how the content will be arranged
- Elaborate on functionality of navigation and suggested layout
- Understand how the project will ultimately be built

All the necessary ideas and elements that go into storyboards are a direct result of the brainstorming sessions discussed in Chapter 1, "Planning Production Before Production."

Before you begin to create storyboards, a meeting of the minds must occur between your design and development team members. During the brainstorming sessions, they must reach a consensus regarding the functionality of the proposed design. The storyboards you are about to build will work directly from the notes and ideas taken from those meetings. If in storyboarding you discover that questions on functionality still arise, this indicates that more brainstorming and planning is needed before you can create viable storyboards.

Consider site navigation, for example. Your storyboards will reflect the following:

- Look and feel
- Element spacing
- Element functionality (are there rollover states for buttons?)
- Animation involved (how it animates; initial animations? ongoing? mouse driven?)
- Action involved (what happens, how it happens, and/or where do you go?)

If you find that you do not have enough information to show everything in this list, it is back to the drawing board. Proper planning will go a long way toward the development of your site. Answering such questions before you begin designing and coding will prevent you from wasting critical budgeted time and dollars on rebuilding elements that may have been doomed from the start. It is always a good idea for design and development to first discuss their thoughts on functionality (due to the differences of each profession). The developer can answer more detailed questions related to backend technology and possible "do's and don'ts" for implementing design in a given timeframe or budget. On the other hand, the design team can answer more visually expressive questions of branding and "look and feel." The two professions compliment each other and should create a dynamic within the team that will support the rest of the production process—going beyond look and feel.

Step 2: Storyboarding the Site

The making of a good storyboard starts with the use of a good storyboard template. A good storyboard template, like the one shown in Figure 2.1, contains ample room for illustrations, sketches, and direction in the stage area. It also provides sections for naming standards, screen size, notes, and version numbers. Other areas to consider when building the template include frames per second, key frame naming, and movie/scene references. You might find these sections useful when building a storyboard. Remember that the storyboard is essentially a blueprint for the team of developers putting together the templates and the rest of the site.

As you learned in the preceding chapter, the brainstorming meetings resulted in the following information screens being planned for the mock employee site:

1. Main Navigation
2. Employee Default Page
3. Professional Biography
4. Personal Biography
5. Skills and Samples
6. In Their Own Words

This information can easily be displayed in two distinct templates. One template will contain the main site navigation and serve as a shell for displaying the employee information pages. The second template will contain the actual employee information pages. The goal here is to create a template that contains a separate scene for each of the different employee information pages. Chapter 4, "Building the Templates," discusses these two templates more thoroughly.

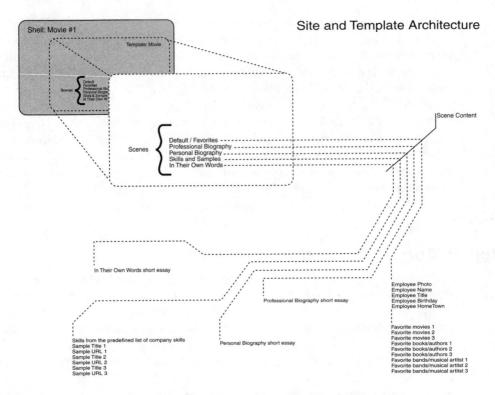

Figure 2.1 *Good storyboarding starts with a good storyboard template.*

The navigation will be best utilized if it acts as a component in a shell that will play host to the employee information. You have a main movie (the host) and an employee movie (the template). Simple enough. To arrange your storyboard, you first determine the order of element display and how the elements will react to user requests. This determination is sometimes referred to as *functionality schematics*. The employee site functionality schematic is shown in the two-template organization in Figure 2.2. These schematics are yet another vital element to the storyboard process. They help plot the direction and flow of the site for an easy understanding of the basic functionality.

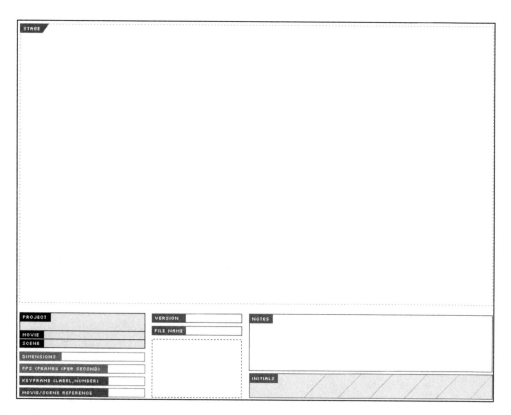

STAGE

PROJECT		VERSION		NOTES
MOVIE		FILE NAME		
SCENE				
DIMENSIONS				
FPS (FRAMES (PER SECOND)				
KEYFRAME (LABEL, NUMBER)				INITIALS
MOVIE/SCENE REFERENCE				

FIGURE 2.2   *Two basic templates are all that is needed in the employee site. Movie 1 template will serve as the shell and contain the main site navigation. Movie 2 contains five separate scenes, one for each of the different employee information pages.*

First, take a look at the employee information template. This template needs to contain additional navigation to each of the areas brought to light during the brainstorming. But how will this navigation work? Well, the easiest way to do this is to have every main category set up as a separate scene.

Each scene should be represented in the schematic showing placement and flow, as mentioned previously. Referencing the notes from the brainstorming sessions, you can see that there are five scenes (employee information pages: an Employee Default Page, a Professional Biography page, a Personal Biography page, a Skills and Samples page, and a In Their Own Words page). These need to be plotted showing the relationship and order intended from the brainstorming notes.

After the order of the site has been established and the concept of navigation flushed out, the storyboards will roll out with ease. Basically each major plot from the schematic should be transferred to the storyboard (with more of a focus on layout than on design at this point).

Although storyboards can be rough sketches on napkins or tissue paper, most clients will respect the fact that you went through the trouble of building it in some type of electronic document such as Adobe Illustrator, Macromedia Freehand, Flash, or even Adobe Acrobat. Although it may be acceptable to pass information in a slipshod manner internally and between team members, the fact of the matter is that storyboards are keystone elements that will be reviewed and referenced by clients and your fellow co-workers. (Did a designer say that?)

> **note**
>
> **Potential Bug.** Both Macromedia Freehand and Adobe Illustrator are excellent to use in conjunction with Flash. However, beware of a slight bug when using Illustrator. When pasting from Illustrator 8 into Flash, sometimes an "EPS Not Understood" error message displays. When this happens, the pasted information takes the shapes of the brush palette default items. It does not happen all the time, but when it does, consider using Freehand instead.

In addition, you want to build production off of these storyboards. The more work you put into them in the planning and storyboarding stage, the more production work you can save yourself in the long run.

While we're on the subject of saving time, if you happen to have access to Macromedia Freehand or Adobe Illustrator, the task of designing for Flash will most definitely be eased. They both export to an SWF movie file. Both allow copy and paste of vector items between Flash and themselves. Utilizing these programs, you can easily transform the storyboards into the final design with little or no effort.

Just remember to set up your Freehand and Illustrator documents to the exact dimensions of the movie and use separate layers for unique items to separate key elements of design.

The only thing left is to tidy up loose ends on the schematic side of things. Then the design is a go! Figures 2.3 through 2.10 show the complete storyboard for the mock employee site.

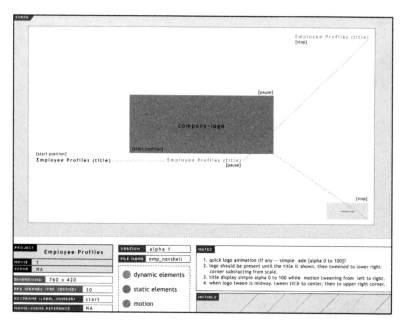

FIGURE 2.3   *Opening splash screen for employee site.*

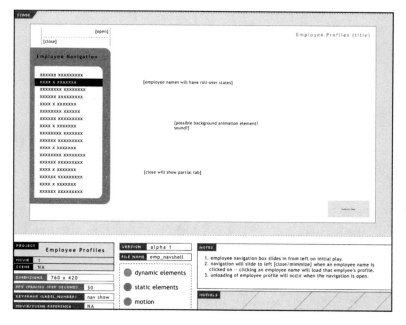

FIGURE 2.4   *The shell template showing the open state of the navigation.*

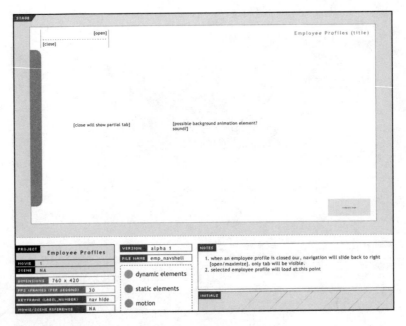

FIGURE 2.5   *The shell template showing the closed state of the navigation.*

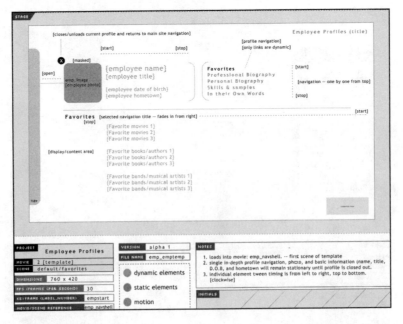

FIGURE 2.6   *Employee information template showing the first scene in the movie: the Employee Default page.*

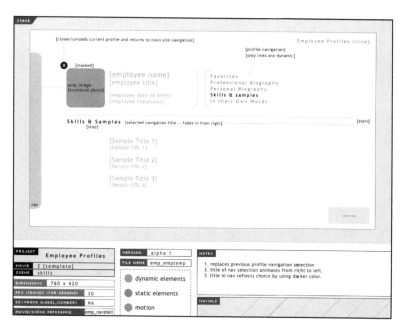

FIGURE 2.7   *Employee information template showing the first scene in the movie: the Skills and Samples page.*

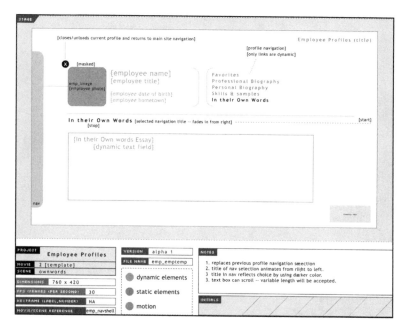

FIGURE 2.8   *Employee information template showing the first scene in the movie: the In Their Own Words page.*

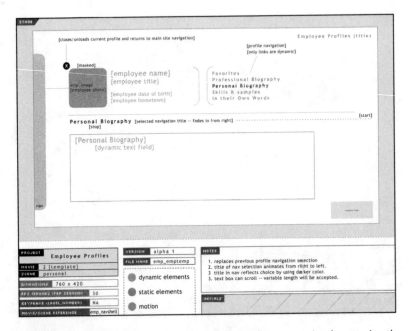

FIGURE 2.9   *Employee information template showing the first scene in the movie: the Personal Biography page.*

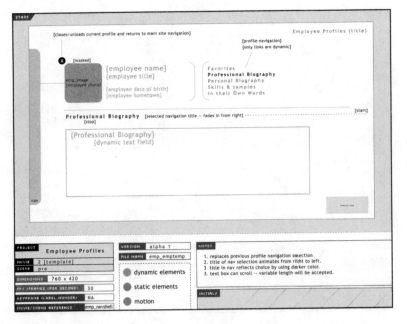

FIGURE 2.10   *Employee information template showing the first scene in the movie: the Professional Biography page.*

The Goals of Site Design

The goals of site design are to establish a stable multipurposed site that reflects the client's wants and site definition while pushing the client's brand further. Storyboards are made up of all the required elements of the site and help to produce a blueprint to build the site. This, in turn, can represent the work to be undertaken.

Site design requires the following rudimentary steps:

1. Organize your ideas.
2. Plot resource allocation.
3. Assess the overall project.
4. Develop a detailed structure.

A good storyboard reflects each of these steps.

Throughout the rest of this book, you will turn to storyboards for information regarding placement, exact functionality (give or take a bit, depending on changes that may arise during production), and overall design and development specifications. As mentioned previously, "issues" may arise along the way relating to flow, functionality, or even design. Storyboards, used as a basic roadmap, will help during those troubled times.

Choreographing Movement and Pace

With a basic storyboard complete, the next step is to start implementing the design in Flash. The almost-always-neglected attributes of Flash design are timing and pace. Timing the movement and positioning the elements are critical to the smoothness of play and the streaming aspect (the pace) of any Flash file. If timed or choreographed poorly, the viewer suffers. The viewer's intended experience will chug along with long pauses between major keyframes or scenes and shuddering animation (quite possibly resulting in a quick exit). Maybe, just maybe, the viewer thinks that their machine has crashed (or worse, it has).

Users often have lesser machines than the persons who develop Flash sites. While looking tremendously cool on a development or design machine, movies just do not play as smoothly on machines with slower processors and, in many cases, slower Internet connections. Machines with overbooked resources will also have a hard time trying to keep up with your studio-quality animation, but that is another story.

Let's go ahead and look at a few pointers that will make your movies roll as smoothly as possible on any machine. In the future, these methods should be attended prior to actual development.

Spacing Elements in Time

One incredibly important factor when developing in Flash is the spacing of elements on the timeline. Believe it or not, this is the cause for most sluggish movies. The reason is that when keyframes stream they are loading in order, from beginning to end. If many keyframes cluster in close proximity to each other on the timeline, either above or below, the download time and playback will be affected.

Suppose that you have an image that animates on the 10th keyframe, for instance, and the animation lasts for 10 frames. At the same time, the accompanying text for the image animates across the screen during those same 10 keyframes. Suppose further that both the image and the text begin at the same point on the timeline, as illustrated in Figure 2.11, although obviously on two different layers. In such a case, Flash will start downloading them both from top to bottom or bottom to top (depending on the load order specified; as discussed in Chapter 4, in more detail) before resuming playback of the movie.

When attempting to solve issues such as those presented in the preceding example, one keyframe's placement can make all the difference. If you position either of the two initial (start) keyframes one to two frames before or after the other, as shown in Figure 2.12, the streaming sequence will flow a bit more smoothly, allowing one element to completely load before attempting to load the next. If there are even more frames between the two, the animation will, of course, flow more smoothly (especially if one animation completes before the next begins).

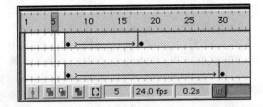

FIGURE 2.11 *With two keyframe's animations occurring at the same time, the streaming sequence may be jarring.*

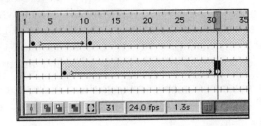

FIGURE 2.12 *A better way to handle two keyframe animations that occur simultaneously.*

This scenario is not the only way to ease the playback of your movie. You could, for example, make symbols of every item that will be reused in different scenes. By doing so you not only reduce file size, you also ease the playback because a symbol needs to be downloaded just one time.

Remember as well that text within Flash can sometimes be a size hog. You can greatly reduce size by using device fonts for static type and by linking movies to font symbols in the library. Take precautions to minimize the size of font characters; otherwise, streaming will more than likely cause playback to halt when it begins to load, especially when it is animated. Avoid animating large text blocks whenever possible.

Last but not least, the frame rate has a lot to do with animation. The chosen frame rate greatly affects the movie's speed.

Transitions

Have you ever been watching television when suddenly your favorite program was interrupted by one of those horrible local commercials? Sadly, it happens to the best of us! Has someone ever grabbed your remote and just kept skimming channels while you waited anxiously? I hate that too! One more, I promise. Have you ever noticed that some programs show the name of the program before going to a commercial break, or play sound bits or theme music when returning? Friends, welcome to the wonderful world of transitions.

Most people do not like quick or abrupt changes in scenery, placement, or thought for that matter. Even though it is not the nature for all of us to be creatures of habit, comfortable transitions in life are more important than most realize.

note

Determining Frame Rate. When determining what frame rate to use, consider these pointers:

- If your movie is made almost entirely of static elements, and almost no animation, a lower setting will do you justice (for example, 10 to 12).

- If your movie has a lot of animation and you intend to keep it looking as smooth as possible, a midsized frame rate will work better. A frame rate of 18 to 24 will play and appear to render more frames during playback, thus creating a smoother animation between keyframes.

- If your work is for highbandwidth display, a much higher frame rate can be applied. For a nice smooth animation, try 32. Of course, you can go higher. If you do so, however, keep in mind that simpler animations work best with higher frame rates. Multiple symbols being tweened at the same time can cause slower processors to chug (as mentioned previously).

The best bet is to use your best judgment. That said, keep these pointers in mind when applying your design. Doing so just might save you a lot of trouble in the long run.

Transitions in Flash help relate the message of change to the user. Design-wise, transitions can inspire more creative and experimental work. You can further reinforce the notion of concept and navigation by using them wisely. Unfortunately, too few sites pull them off well. This is not to say that there should be transitions for every element in your movie, or that everything should animate—that approach would just be annoying.

With the employee site, marking where and when the transitions will occur on the storyboard design notes will not only make presentation easier, it also will speed production. It will enable you to keep on track with the projects and time allotted.

Because the employee site will have scenes, transitions are a given. They will help tie the main movie to the template and reinforce a feeling of togetherness that would otherwise be nonexistent with a static site.

The storyboards show how the navigation moves out of the way to allow for the employee template movie to load into place. This creates an easy transition to adhere to while revealing to the audience that something is about to happen. When the employee template is loaded, it will have lead-in animation to resolve placement of objects (as opposed to just plopping them down in front of the user).

Remember the following when planning your transitions:

1. Will they make sense to you and to the client?
2. Will they be in scope with the project?
3. What will remain stationary during the transitions?
4. Will they live up to the original concept?
5. Could they be used to help playback and to organize the streaming of movies based on file size?

Planning transitions in Flash is basically taking into account the method mentioned previously (spacing), and the goal of the intended design. Also, making your client happy is a good thing to keep in mind.

Finally, while developing the transitions, keep in mind that all design elements should be represented on the storyboard. Aside from being "designed," the employee site will be created using dynamic content. These dynamic areas deserve special attention because they are the reason for the templates. (See Figure 2.13.)

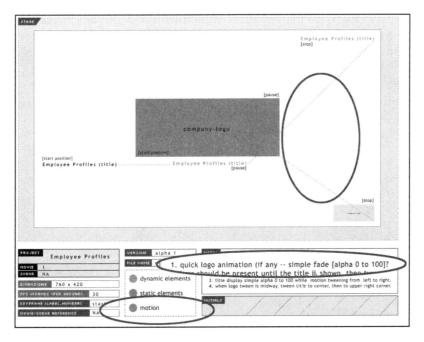

FIGURE 2.13   *The storyboards show and describe transitions through illustration, color, and notes.*

Dynamic Versus Static Design

When developing the storyboards and the design of the employee site, dynamic elements and static elements should be clearly spec'd out (as mentioned earlier). The main reason to mark the dynamic areas differently from static elements is to acknowledge that they are present and to help visually distinguish changing elements of content from the rest of the design. Basically, the template is the bowl, the static elements are the presentation, and the dynamic elements are the soup. Dynamic elements also can be "the presentation": More often than not, however, they tend to be characterized as the core content of a site. Dynamic elements in your template are those variable placeholders for values that will be updated with real content from your database that you will create in the next chapter. Static elements are the pieces in the template that remain constant for every movie generated.

By marking them clearly within curly brackets (which, by the way, is how you will determine a Generator variable), blocking them with specific color, or just greeking the text will help identify these elements for the storyboard and further development. How they are marked is completely up to you.

However the dynamic elements are mocked up, a specific method should apply across the board so that anyone working on the project can easily recognize them. In the storyboards that you just created, for example, dynamic elements appear within the curly braces { } (see Figure 2.14). This advice applies especially to designers because the animation, transitions, and overall look and feel depend on the placement of dynamic elements. Remember also that by keeping these elements marked consistently, production will flow more easily.

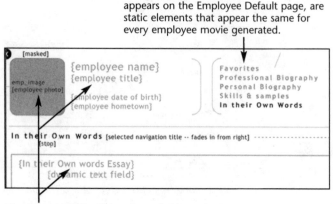

Navigation elements, such as the one that appears on the Employee Default page, are static elements that appear the same for every employee movie generated.

The text within the { } are dynamic elements that change for each employee movie generated.

FIGURE 2.14 *Storyboarding dynamic and static elements.*

Suppose, for instance, that the entire design is completed in Flash, and the transitions are finished as well. What would happen if the elements you have moving around do not need to move around? What if elements that were thought to be static were actually supposed to be dynamic? These questions are typical of Web design in general and are quite often asked during the zero hour of a tight deadline.

Take time in the beginning to understand how a site will function before building it and all will be well. You will soon be on to your next successful project!

Chapter Summary

In this chapter you learned that storyboards are crucial to site planning. They serve as the foundation for the design and development of the templates and, ultimately, the final site. As a blueprint, storyboards

1. Describe the key elements to be included in the design.
2. Show how to choreograph movement and pace of animations.
3. Display the spacing and placement of static and dynamic elements.
4. Describe the movie and scene transitions.

With the brainstorming sessions finished and the subsequent storyboards that resulted from those meetings created, the necessary planning phase of the project is complete. Throughout the development of the mock employee site in the remaining chapters, you will see how these first two planning steps in the workflow process play a necessary and important role. Think of this project as a building. In such case, these initial steps lay the foundation for the rest of the structure. Ask any architect and he will tell you that no one in his right mind would begin construction without first laying down a foundation! These planning steps will support the rest of the project by defining how elements of the site work and look. More importantly, thorough planning enables you to consider all questions and solutions carefully. Successful planning means you never have to rethink and rebuild.

Now that you understand the importance of planning and preparation, you are ready to begin work on the three key elements that make up the workflow process: the database, the template, and the data-entry tool. Chapter 3, "Developing the Database," introduces you to the makings of the database. In Chapter 4, you begin putting the template together. Then in Chapter 5, "The Data-Entry Tool," you create the data-entry tool.

In this chapter, you learned many behind-the-scenes lessons about creating and designing site storyboards, the blueprints of high-content Flash sites. What started as brainstorming ideas was refined and structured in your storyboards. The Flash templates were certainly influenced by the storyboards because they illustrated design, placement, and flow. They also supplied important guidelines for interface elements and visual transitions. Static content and dynamic content were crafted and defined in the planning and development of the storyboards.

CHAPTER 3

Developing the Database

Introduction

With the necessary and important part of planning in the preceding chapters complete, you are now ready to begin the actual development of the employee site. You begin by constructing the central element in the process, the database. Along the way you will learn the concepts that go into the development of database design and implementation as you construct the employee database. The database is one of three key elements that make up the workflow process for building sites with offline Generator. Together with the template and the data-entry tool, you have a complete set of tools for building dynamic sites with Generator.

In particular, this chapter covers the following topics:

- Learning database terminology
- Determining what database best suits your project
- Defining data fields in your database
- Building the employee database
- Formatting a data source for Generator
- Constructing SQL queries for extracting data from the database

Site building is very much a team effort. The employee site is no different. Brainstorming meetings were conducted with as many team members from various disciplines as possible. The storyboards were also put together as a team effort.

Databases 101: Tables, Records, and Fields (Oh My!)

Before delving into the details of designing and implementing a database that will be used as the foundation for the employee Web site, you must understand a few key concepts that are used as a basis throughout the rest of this chapter.

All databases, at a minimum, support the following types of entities: fields, records, and tables.

A *field* is a container for a discrete unit of information stored within a database. In addition to the actual information stored in a field, a set of attributes is associated with the field that describes the information it contains. Although the set of attributes associated with fields varies slightly across database packages, some attributes are universal. The two most important of these universal attributes are field name and field type. A *field name* is a logical identifier through which a field's contained information can be accessed. A *field type* qualifies a field's contained information for data-handling purposes. Some common field types include integer, date, and string.

A collection of fields related in some way is referred to as a *record*. For example, a record describing an employee might consist of three fields: last name, first name, and hometown.

Finally, a *table* acts as a container for a collection of similarly structured records. In fact, a table is actually defined by a set of field definitions that fully describe the records of information stored within it. Furthermore, attributes are associated with tables in the same way they are associated with fields. The two most important universal attributes for tables are the table name and primary key. A *table name* is a logical identifier through which a table's contained records can be accessed. A *primary key* is a subset of the field definitions that comprise a table definition that can be used to uniquely identify any one of the records contained in a table. In a relational database, every table is required to have a unique key as part of its definition.

Here's an example that brings all these concepts together. This example uses three fields to describe an employee: last name, first name, and hometown. These three fields will comprise the definition of a table that will store employee information for a company.

Table 3.1 Employees

Field Name	Field Type
last_name	string
first_name	string
hometown	string

One last thing to do: Specify a primary key for the Employees table. Here's why. Looking at the information that will be stored in the table, there doesn't seem to be a collection of fields that is guaranteed to uniquely identify any record stored in the table. In other words, it's quite possible that two employees in the same company may have the same first and last name and also come from the same hometown.

An easy way to overcome this minor obstacle is to add one more field to the table definition. This field will be used specifically to uniquely identify any given record stored in the table.

Table 3.2 Employees

Field Name	Field Type
employee_id (primary key)	integer
last_name	string
first_name	string
hometown	string

In this example, the employee_id field was added to the table definition and designated as the table's primary key. As each new employee's information is added to the table, a unique integer value will be associated with the record and can be used to uniquely identify that record within the table.

A little later in this chapter, you will learn more about these concepts and how they are used in a relational database (during the discussion of an actual implementation of the employee site database). For now, however, it is important to take a closer look at how Generator provides access to data in general.

Generator/Flash 5 Data Sources

Generator's real power derives from its capability to produce dynamic multimedia content based on the interaction of templates with well-defined data sources. *Generator templates* are essentially a collection of placeholders for atomic multimedia elements such as text, images, and sound. Placeholders within templates are assigned to data sources that provide a link to actual content.

Generator provides a great deal of flexibility in what it accepts as a data source. In fact, there is such a degree of flexibility that what you decide to use as a data source is, for the most part, arbitrary. The caveat is that Generator (or more specifically, the objects you utilize within Generator) must be able to understand how to handle the information provided to it by a data source.

Basically, the format in which data sources must provide information to Generator is as a comma-delimited list of values. Generator understands how to work with two types of comma-delimited lists: Name/Value pairs and Column Name/Value Collections. Name/Value pairs are lists that have one value per variable. Column Name/Value Collections are lists where one or more values can be associated with the associated variable.

A good example of a Column Name/Value Collection is a short list of employee statistics such as last name, first name, and hometown. In a list with more than one employee, each of these fields would have as many values associated with them as there are employees. The example that follows shows you how you would format such a collection of variables and values for Generator.

> EMPLOYEEID, lastName, firstName, hometown
>
> "1", "Borucki", "Anthony", "Gurney"
>
> "2", "Groch", "Matthew", "Wood Dale"
>
> "3", "Mohamed", "Imran", "Long Grove"
>
> "4", "Posso", "Carlos", "Chicago"

> **note**
>
> **Data Sources.** A data source in Generator can be a collection of static values hard-coded into a Generator template, a URL (supported protocols include HTTP, FTP, FILE, JDBC/ODBC, and a Java class that implements an interface defined by Generator. As long as any of these data sources provide information in a recognizable comma-delimited format, Generator can work with them. When you look at it this way, the actual data sources available to Generator can be seen as arbitrary, particularly with respect to the option of being able to use Java classes.

Note that the first record contains a comma-delimited list of four values indicating the column names of the table and that each of the succeeding records contains comma-delimited lists of values corresponding to those column names.

With the different types of data sources available for development of the employee site, which one should you use?

Keeping in mind that one of the primary goals in producing the employee Web site is to provide a dynamic forum through which Big International Company can become acquainted with your staff. You can immediately discard the option of using hard-coded static values as a data source. Hard-coding static values into Generator templates is certainly useful for providing information that is seldom updated; in the case of the employee site, however, you need something with a little more flexibility.

Why the focus on data source flexibility? Imagine that the decision was made to go ahead and use hard-coded static values as the data source of choice for the employee site. Every time an addition or modification to a particular employee's information is required, the Generator templates incorporating those data sources must be updated. It's not hard to see how this would become a maintenance nightmare.

To avoid this situation and maximize the flexibility of your data-source type of choice, employ a concept commonly referred to as abstraction. In the context of an information system (such as the employee site), *abstraction* is a mechanism through which an information "consumer" obtains data from a corresponding information "provider" in an indirect manner such that a change in the immediate provider of data does not have an impact on the information consumer. The primary advantage that abstraction provides is that overall maintenance of an information system can be minimized—and all information systems, especially Web sites, invariably require maintenance.

To illustrate this point, there is no layer of abstraction between a Generator template (the information consumer) and a data source of hard-coded static values (the information provider). A change in the data provided by this type of data source requires a corresponding change in the template itself. On the other hand, any of the other data source types supported by Generator create a layer of abstraction between a template and the data provided to it by the data source because a change in the data would not require a corresponding update in the template.

When choosing a data source type that provides the maximum flexibility for dynamic Web site requirements, you can probably rule out FTP and FILE URLs as well. Although they both provide more flexibility as a data source than hard-coded static values, both of these protocols imply accessing data stored within text files. Although this type of data source might be acceptable in some circumstances, the data source that you choose for the employee site will need to be able to handle data updates coming from multiple employees at the same time. File systems, for the most part, do not readily support this sort of behavior.

HTTP URLs, on the other hand, are definitely a viable option as a data-source type. Traditionally, HTTP URLs imply a static file similar to that of FTP and FILE URLs. With the current capabilities of today's Web servers, however, HTTP URLs are an incredibly flexible data source, particularly when they refer to server-side scripts.

Generator's JDBC/ODBC URL data source type is also fairly flexible in that it provides direct connectivity to a SQL-compliant data source (such as a relational database). However, this data-source type suffers from the same disadvantages inherent in using hard-coded static values in that any kind of change in the underlying structure of the SQL-compliant data source would require an update to the incorporating template as well. Of course, this data-source type could just as easily be used to point to something known as a stored procedure, which would effectively eliminate this disadvantage. A stored procedure is a common database object that usually contains a program invoked to retrieve and/or manipulate data. Although the use of stored procedures provides the flexibility you are looking for in a data-source type, the following factors put this data-source type at a relative disadvantage:

- They are not very portable from the database for which they were originally written.
- They add an extra element of programming complexity and maintenance to the development equation.

Java classes implement a well-defined interface and are the final data-source type to consider. Because of the range of functionality that the Java language provides, this data-source type could be considered the most flexible option of all. Because of the time constraints associated with producing the employee Web site, however, the learning curve associated with utilizing Java data sources puts this option at a disadvantage when compared to accessing server-side scripts through HTTP URLs.

Based on this analysis, move forward with an implementation of the employee Web site on the assumption that HTTP URLs will be used as the data-source type of choice within Generator. Furthermore, assume that the HTTP URLs will reference server-side scripts that interact with a relational database to provide all dynamic content to the Web site. The combination of these design decisions provide the following benefits:

- A flexible data source that minimizes Web site maintenance costs
- A low learning curve associated with using a scripting language rather than Java
- The capability to allow concurrent updates to the Web site data through the use of a relational database

Databases

Although many databases are available for use in developing dynamic Web sites, take care to match the database you eventually decide on with the functional requirements and time/budget constraints of your project. In the case of the employee Web site, you are already aware of the following factors:

1. **Functional requirements.** The employee Web site is intended to functionally serve as an introduction of your staff to Big International Company. Between your staff members providing their personal information for the Web site and Big International Company actually visiting the Web site once it is complete, the volume of traffic that the database will have to handle will most likely be very light.

2. **Time constraints of the project.** As mentioned before, you have less than a month to deliver the employee Web site. With that being the case, you want to choose a database package with the lowest learning curve with respect to implementation and maintenance.

3. **Budget constraints of the project.** Budget constraints are always a factor in any project. Because this is a relatively small-scale project with minimal functional requirements, consider a database package that not only addresses the other factors you are considering but also comes at a relatively low cost.

Based on these factors, the following sections review a set of widely used databases that span the spectrums of cost and performance and then identify the most viable candidate.

Access

Access is Microsoft's entry-level relational database offering. Access has proven itself invaluable to developers as a database solution addressing small business problems. This is most likely because the package itself is well-rounded in its feature set, very easy to learn and use, and nearly as ubiquitous as Microsoft Office (through which it is most often distributed).

SQL Server

SQL Server is Microsoft's enterprise-class relational database-management system. SQL Server is usually incorporated into medium-to-large business solutions that address relatively complex business problems. SQL Server is an ideal candidate as a database in systems where a large feature set and good performance are being measured against license costs.

Oracle

Oracle is the de facto industry standard enterprise-class relational database management system for very large, heavy-traffic information sites. For corporations that are developing these types of high-performance systems and have a sizable budget to match, Oracle is usually the first in a short list of candidates. As a real-world example, the popular Britannica.com Web site is built on top of an Oracle database.

Database RAD Tools

A number of tools are commercially available to developers to facilitate the rapid development of their applications. Because nearly every practical application relies on a database, these Rapid Application Development (RAD) tools provide application developers with controls through which the complexities of database interaction are masked.

For the most part, each of these RAD tools fundamentally provides similar feature sets, especially in terms of quickly developing Web-based applications. The following sections quickly review some of the more popular RAD tools currently on the market and their feature sets (particularly as they pertain to database connectivity).

Macromedia Dreamweaver UltraDev

Macromedia Dreamweaver UltraDev is a visual development environment targeted at nontechnical Web developers who want to incorporate relatively simple database connectivity into their Web sites. For the most part, this connectivity is provided through an intuitive drag-and-drop interface that enables Web developers to graphically associate fields within a database with Web page elements.

With respect to developing database-driven Web sites, UltraDev's most notable feature is its capability to show live data within its editing environment. From a development standpoint, this is a very convenient feature that can certainly facilitate the rapid development of most Web-based applications. Furthermore, UltraDev will automatically generate database connectivity scripts associated with your Web site in a variety of formats, including ASP, JSP, and CFML (a little more on that in the next section). In fact, through a plug-in provided by UnifyEwave, UltraDev can interact with Java-based server-side components to provide even more complex dynamic Web site behavior.

Macromedia ColdFusion

Macromedia ColdFusion is a complete Web application server tool that runs concurrently in most Windows and Solaris Web server environments. Its suite of visual tools, server technology, and open language environment (known as ColdFusion Markup Language, or CFML) all work toward expediting the Web application development process, from implementation to development.

As a scripting language, CFML supports more than 70 server-side elements, 200 functions, and 800 third-party components. Additionally, ColdFusion supports Java and C++ and fully integrates with object-transaction middleware components.

Microsoft Visual Interdev

Visual Interdev is Microsoft's integrated development environment (IDE) targeted at Web-based application development. Visual Interdev will soon disappear, however, and its functionality will be incorporated into various tools within another of Microsoft's products, Visual Studio.net.

Currently, Visual Interdev provides visual design tools for creating Active Server Pages that can interact with middle-tier components and databases. Besides its visually oriented toolset, another of Visual InterDev's strengths lies in its capability to produce finished Web pages that can support a variety of Web browser platforms.

Server-Side Scripting

Server-side scripting differs from client-side scripting (such as JavaScript) in that server-side scripts are executed on the Web server. Because script execution is local to the Web server, server-side scripting provides a great deal more power and flexibility to Web developers in general. This is most readily reflected in the ability of server-side scripts to retrieve information from databases, make decisions based on that information, and then finally deliver dynamic Web site content.

The following sections briefly review some of the server-side scripting languages currently being used by Web developers to provide dynamic Web site content with a particular emphasis being placed on Active Server Pages (ASP).

ASP

ASP is a server-side scripting format from Microsoft that combines HTML with the functionality provided through a variety of scripting languages, most notably VBScript and JScript, to produce dynamic Web content. Scripts written with ASP can be further extended by interacting with COM components to do things such as access information stored in a database.

An ASP script is utilized in a Web environment by writing the script and saving it as a text file with an .ASP extension. As Web browsers send requests to the Web server hosting the script file, the Web server realizes that it must process the script by virtue of the requested file's .ASP extension. The Web server then loads the script and executes its instructions and creates an HTML Web page that is sent to the requesting Web browser.

Let's start with some basics.

VBScript must be encapsulated within delimiters:

```
<% ="Hello world!" %>
```

Here's how that would look in an actual ASP page that displays the text Hello world! (see Figure 3.1):

```
<@ Language="VBScript" @>
<html>
<head>
<title>An example using ASP</title>
</head>
<body>
<% = "Hello world!" %>
</body>
```

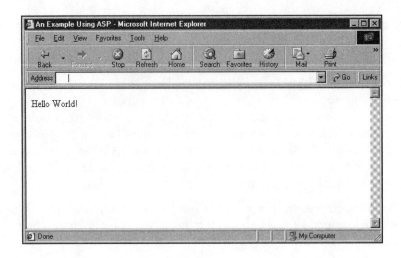

FIGURE 3.1   *The simple ASP page displayed through Internet Explorer.*

Moving on to more powerful features, ASP has a set of objects that are intrinsically associated with it to provide functions for getting and sending information to a Web client, interacting with the Web server, handling session management, and so forth. Sending information to a Web client is simple enough. You already saw a very simple example of doing that. Here's an alternative way to use one of ASP's intrinsic objects, Response:

```
<@ Language="VBScript" @>
<html>
<head>
<title>Another example using ASP</title>
</head>
<body>
<% Response.Write "Hello world!" %>
</body>
```

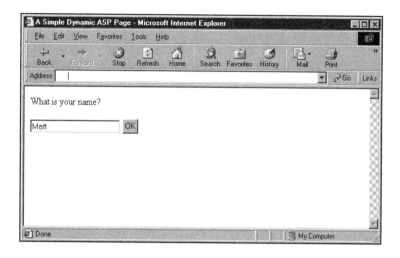

FIGURE 3.2   *The dynamic ASP page displayed through Internet Explorer.*

You can begin to see how Web sites provide dynamic content by taking a look at another intrinsic ASP object: Request. The Request object enables you to get information from a Web client that has been submitted through a form. After you have the ability to receive input from a Web client, you can use that information to make decisions and respond accordingly. (See Figure 3.2) The following example of an ASP file named HELLO.ASP illustrates this point:

```
<@ Language="VBScript" @>
<html>
<head>
<title>A simple dynamic ASP page</title>
</head>
<body>
<%
If IsEmpty(Request.Form("name")) Then
Response.Write "What is your name?"
%>
<form action="Hello.asp" method="post">
<input name="name" type="textbox">
<input type="submit" value="OK">
</form>
<%
Else
Response.Write "Hello, " & Request.Form("name") & "!"
End If
%>
</body>
```

From these examples, you can begin to see how the employee Web site can be constructed. The main page would list all the employees and the user would select one and click a button to request the employee's personal information. The page that would display the selected employee's information would know exactly what information to retrieve from the database and render as output because it would have received the selected employee's unique ID as form-based input.

PHP

PHP (PHP: Hypertext Preprocessor) is a server-side scripting language like ASP. It shares a similar feature set with most other server-side scripting languages in that it can dynamically generate Web page content, interact with cookies, work with form data, and so forth.

However, PHP has a couple of features that make it unique as a scripting language. First, it natively supports a very large number of commercially available databases, thus making it simple for Web developers to incorporate database connectivity into their Web sites. Second, it natively supports a wide variety of service protocols beyond that of HTTP and also can handle direct socket communication.

The following is a rendition of the classic Hello World! message in PHP:

```
<html>
<head>
<title>A Simple PHP Example</title>
<body>
<?php echo "Hello world!"; ?>
</body>
</html>
```

JSP

JSP (Java Server Pages) also is a server-side scripting language that is very similar to ASP. JSP is a part of the Java 2 Enterprise Edition (J2EE) platform and is meant to provide the power and flexibility of the Java programming language to Web development through a relatively easy-to-learn script format.

If you're interested in learning more about JSP technology, a good place to start is at **http://java.sun.com/products/jsp/index.html**.

Tcl

Tcl (Tool Command Language) is an embeddable command language, meaning that the basic language kernel is designed to be embedded within arbitrary applications and utilized as a mechanism for integrating application-specific functionality.

The implications of such a language are very interesting, particularly in the context of providing richer, more dynamic Web site experiences by just embedding Tcl within traditionally static constructs such as HTML, as an obvious example.

The Future: XML

Before concluding this section on Generator data sources, it is important to take a moment to discuss one last technology currently making a huge impact on the way information is being communicated: XML.

XML, or eXtensible Markup Language, is a markup language that is very similar in structure and content to HTML. XML is referred to as extensible because XML tags can be arbitrarily defined, unlike in HTML in which all tags come predefined. At its most fundamental level, XML is designed to provide a mechanism through which data can be both fully described and logically organized. In fact, this should sound vaguely familiar to the way in which database entities were described at the beginning of this chapter—structures that organize and qualify data.

To a Web developer, the best way to get introduced to the technical details of XML is with a working example. The following example reuses the example of an employee record consisting of a last name, first name, and hometown fields:

```xml
<?xml version="1.0"?>
<employees>
<employee id="30">
<lastName>Borucki</lastName>
<firstName>Anthony</firstName>
<hometown>Gurney</hometown>
</employee>
<employee id="24">
<lastName>Groch</lastName>
<firstName>Matthew</firstName>
<hometown>Wood Dale</hometown>
</employee>
<employee id="26">
<lastName>Mohamed</lastName>
<firstName>Imran</firstName>
<hometown>Long Grove</hometown>
</employee>
<employee id="28">
<lastName>Posso</lastName>
<firstName>Carlos</firstName>
<hometown>Chicago</hometown>
</employee>
</employees>
```

Now take a look at some of the basic technical aspects of XML by walking through this example document.

The first line of any XML document contains the XML declaration, which indicates the version of the XML specification to which the documents conforms. Note that the declaration is not considered to be an element of XML documents and is therefore not subject to the rules applied to all XML elements.

```
<?xml version="1.0"?>
```

The next line in the preceding example document introduces several XML element rules. First of all, note that in the document, each element has a closing tag. This is a requirement of the XML specification (and one of the key deviations from HTML). Second, note that all elements are well nested. In other words, the end tag of an element will always be encountered in an XML document before the start tag of another. Third, all XML documents must have a root tag (in this example, it is the employees tag).

```
<employees>
...
</employees>
```

The next line contains an XML tag with an attribute called id. In XML, all attribute values must be quoted.

```
<employee id="30">
```

The next line illustrates how XML tags are case sensitive. The letter capitalization pattern in the begin tag must exactly match in the end tag of an XML element.

```
<lastName>Borucki</lastName>
```

The rest of the example XML document pretty much conforms to these very simple rules. For a more thorough understanding of XML and its applications, begin your research by visiting **www.xml.org**.

You can utilize XML's rich capacity for describing data with the XML Generator object created by Mike Chambers. He has even provided the source code with it. Find out all there is to know about using XML as a data source at **www.markme.com/generator/XMLColumn.jsp**.

The fact that XML has a rich capacity for describing data has not been lost on the information technology industry and there is clearly a wide acceptance in applying XML across a variety of business situations, particularly in the facilitation of communication between disparate information systems.

Organizing Data

Now that you have had a brief glance at how Generator can interact with data sources to obtain dynamic content, it is time to start thinking about a practical implementation of a database that will be used to store all dynamic information for the employee Web site.

To begin, put together a list of all the information you want to maintain in the database. The elements that you identified in the brainstorming session and then incorporated in the storyboards are the kind of elements you are looking for in this exercise. Once again, proper planning like the first two steps in the workflow process will greatly speed up your work. Not only that, you will find that the work you do is more accurate. To get things started, formally define all the employee information fields.

On a conceptual level, the Web site will provide three categories of information about each employee: demographics (for instance, last name, first name, title), a professional biography, and a personal biography. First, list these fields and, for each field, indicate whether a single value or multiple values may be associated with its definition:

- Last name (single value)
- First name (single value)
- Title (single value)
- Birth date (single value)
- Hometown (single value)
- Email address (single value)
- Photo (single value)
- Favorite movies (multiple values)
- Favorite books (multiple values)
- Favorite bands (multiple values)
- Skills (multiple values)
- Work samples (multiple values)
- Professional biography (single value)
- Personal biography (single value)
- Personal note (single value)

Now that you have a complete list of all the fields that will be stored in the employee database, you need to decide how these fields will be organized into tables.

It should be fairly obvious that the most inefficient way to organize these fields is to put them all into a single table. You have two types of fields: fields that have only one value associated with them, and fields that have multiple values associated with them. If you were to place both field types into a single table, you would be forcing a limitation on the database implementation at the outset because you would have to decide, at design time, the maximum number of values that could be associated with any one of these multivalued fields.

With that being the case, you can immediately see that all multivalued fields should exist in their own tables. Similarly, you can conclude that all single-valued fields can be collectively organized into a single table. In fact, because you know that an individual record of these single-value fields can be associated with any individual staff member (for instance, no staff member has more than one name or more than one birth date), you can probably use this table containing the single-valued fields as the "anchor" table to which all the tables containing multivalued fields will be associated.

Based on these conclusions, organize the fields into their respective tables. As part of this exercise, also determine each field's type as being either an integer, a string, or a date. (This will keep things simple for this practical example.)

Table: Employees

- Last name (string)
- First name (string)
- Title (string)
- Birth date (date)
- Hometown (string)
- Email address (string)
- Photo (string)
- Professional biography (string)
- Personal biography (string)
- Personal note (string)

Next, define the tables that store an employee's favorite movies, books, and bands. One of these tables, Favorite Types, will be used to enumerate the different types of favorites that will be displayed on the employee Web site (for instance, movies, books, or bands). The other table, Favorites, will be used to store the employee-provided descriptions of their favorites, listed in order of importance.

> **note**
>
> **Photo File.** In this initial pass at the Employees table definition, notice that the photo field is defined as a string. In lieu of actually storing the photo image within the database itself, assume that the photo image is being stored as a physical file in the file system of the Web site's server. The photo field will contain a file URL indicating the location of this physical image file.

Table: Favorite Types

- Favorite type description (string)

Table: Favorites

- List order (integer)
- Favorite description (string)

The remaining tables to store skills and work samples are relatively trivial to define:

Table: Skills

- Skill description (string)

Table: Samples

- Work sample URL (string)

Relationships

Now that you have had an initial pass at the table definitions for the employee database, map out how they all relate to one another. Begin with the "anchor" table, the Employees table.

Table: Employees

- Employee ID (integer)
- Last name (string)
- First name (string)
- Title (string)
- Birth date (date)
- Hometown (string)
- Email address (integer)
- Photo (string)
- Professional biography (string)
- Personal biography (string)
- Personal note (string)

Note the Employee ID field at the top of the fields list. As discussed in the introductory section on databases, each table in a relational database requires a primary key definition that can uniquely identify each record stored in a table. Because it is theoretically possible that two employees can have the exact same information in each field in the Employees table, the employee ID field is used as the table's primary key.

Next, re-evaluate the definition of the Favorites table.

First of all, you need to be able to associate a record describing an employee's favorite things with the actual employee. Remember that individual employees are described in the Employees table and that any employee can be uniquely identified in this table through his or her employee ID. Based on that, you can conclude that you need to incorporate an employee ID field into the definition of the Favorites table to establish this association.

Second, you need to be able to qualify each employee's favorite things as being either a favorite movie, book, or band. This can be accomplished by drawing an association between the Favorites and Favorite Types tables similar to the way you are establishing an association between the Favorites and Employees tables.

Table: Favorite Types

- Favorite type ID (integer)
- Favorite type description (string)

Table: Favorites

- Favorite type ID (integer)
- List order (integer)
- Employee ID (integer)
- Favorite description (string)

Note that in the updated definition of the Favorites table, any single record can be uniquely identified through a combination of the values in the favorite type ID, list order, and employee ID fields. In other words, no employee will ever have two number-one favorite movies, books, or bands.

This collection of fields that can be used to uniquely identify any record in the Favorites table can be referred to as a compound primary key because it is comprised of multiple fields (rather than just one as you have seen so far).

Using the design rules outlined in the second pass of defining the Employee, Favorites, and Favorite Types tables, you can go ahead and redefine the remaining tables of the employee database.

Table: Skills

- List order (integer)
- Employee ID (integer)
- Skill description (string)

Table: Samples

- List order (integer)
- Employee ID (integer)
- Work sample URL (string)

Information Architecture

So, although all the information that will be delivered through the employee Web site has been neatly organized into a set of related tables in a database, does this organization really provide any tangible benefits from the perspective of Web application development?

The answer, of course, is yes. What you have done in the database design is lay the groundwork for an intrinsic element of information architecture known as referential integrity. Basically, referential integrity guarantees that the relationships between records in associated tables remain valid.

You can use the current table definitions of Employees and Favorites to illustrate the concept of referential integrity. In essence, it does not make sense for a Favorites record to exist if it is not associated with an employee. This commonsense rule is adhered to in two ways. First, records cannot be added to the Favorites table unless they are associated with a record in the Employees table. Second, a record in the Employees table cannot be deleted if there are records in the Favorites table that are associated with the employee because to do so would create a situation where Favorites records existed without a corresponding employee.

How is referential integrity actually achieved? Well, you have already been introduced to the concept of a primary key. Referential integrity now introduces the concept of a foreign key.

A *foreign key* is a collection of one or more fields in a table that establishes a relationship with another table by referring to the primary key of that table. In the case of the relationship between the Employees and Favorites tables, the employee ID field in the Favorites table is a foreign key. This foreign key establishes a relationship with the Employees table through the primary key of the Employees table: employee ID.

Step 3: Building the Database

Now that the database for the employee Web site is designed on a conceptual level, it's time to implement it.

Based on a brief analysis of some of the relational database packages available on the market, covered earlier, it makes most sense to implement the database design with Microsoft Access for several reasons. First of all, the functional requirements of the employee Web site have already been stated to be relatively light. In other words, complex database queries are probably not going to be submitted to the underlying database by hundreds of concurrent clients such as would be expected for, say, an online securities trading site. Second, Microsoft Access is the simplest of the previously-mentioned database packages to learn, develop with, and maintain. Third, Microsoft Access is, by far and away, the most cost-effective database package solution to implement in terms of absolute dollars. In fact, you may already have Microsoft Access installed on your system as part of the Microsoft Office suite of applications.

With these reasons measured against the goals of the employee Web site, Microsoft Access becomes the obvious choice for the employee database design implementation.

Sample Employee Database

To begin implementation of the employee database design, launch Microsoft Access. For the purposes of this example, it is assumed that Microsoft Access 2000 is the specific version of the product being used.

On startup of Access, you receive the prompt shown in Figure 3.3.

FIGURE 3.3   *From this dialog box, you can open a new or existing Microsoft Access database.*

Choose to create a new, blank Access database and click the OK button. Another dialog box appears prompting you for the filename to assign to the new database (see Figure 3.4).

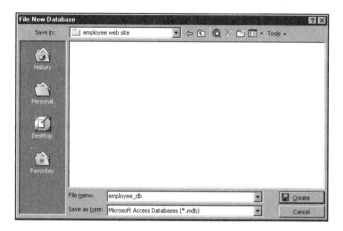

FIGURE 3.4   *You can specify the filename of the new database from this dialog box.*

Type **employee_db** and click the OK button. An empty Access database is created and saved as EMPLOYEE_DB.MDB. Next, the database manager window appears. (See Figure 3.5.)

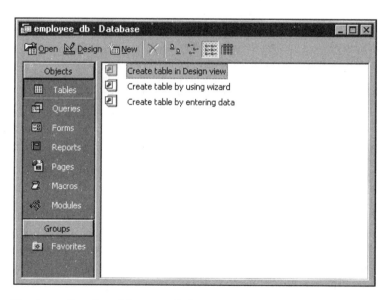

FIGURE 3.5   *The Access Database Manager window.*

You can view all the objects associated with your database through the Database Manager window. Note the menu bar on the left side of the manager window provides an indication of the objects that Access supports: tables, queries, forms, reports, Web pages, macros, and VBA (Visual Basic for Applications) code modules. The right side of the manager window lists the collection of object instances of the type currently selected in the left side.

For the implementation of the employee database, you will work only with table objects. Double-click the first right-side item to begin defining the first table in the employee database. The design view of a new table object appears.

Figure 3.6 illustrates a nearly complete definition of the Employees table. Note a few things about the Access-specific implementation of the table definition.

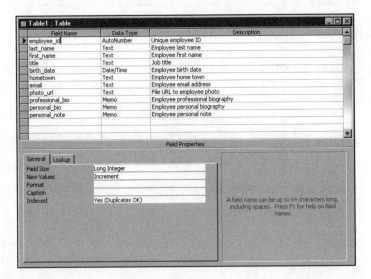

FIGURE 3.6   *This is the Design View window for the Employees table.*

First, the data type of the employee_id field is selected as AutoNumber. In Access, a field type of AutoNumber indicates a numeric field (in this case, a long integer) that by default, starts with a value of 0. Every time a new record is added to the table, the AutoNumber field value is incremented by 1 and assigned to the new record. The first record in the Employees table will have an employee_id of 1, the next record will have an employee_id of 2, and so on.

Second, the Access data type of Text is synonymous with the conceptual design field type of string. In Access, text fields can contain up to 255 ASCII characters.

Third, per the conceptual design of the Employees table, the birth date field has a data type of Date/Time. For your reference, the integer data type in the conceptual design becomes the Number data type as realized in Access.

Fourth and finally, the professional_bio, personal_bio, and personal_note fields have a data type of Memo. As already mentioned, the Text data type will only allow a maximum of 255 ASCII characters. It is not unreasonable, however, to believe that employees might want to author either biography or personal notes that exceed this 255 character limit. Therefore, the professional_bio, personal_bio, and personal_note fields have been defined as a memo field, where a memo field is allowed to contain, for the most part, up to 64,000 characters, which should more than suffice for the purposes of the employee Web site.

The last remaining action to perform in defining the Employees table is to specify the primary key and to save the table definition.

To specify the primary key of a table in Access, just highlight the collection of fields (these are table definition rows in the design view we are using) that comprise the primary key and then click the Primary Key toolbar button (a button with a yellow key centered on its face). In the case of the Employees table, the employee_id has been highlighted and selected as the primary key. Fields that are members of the primary key collection for a table are labeled with a key icon beside their field name. (See Figure 3.7.)

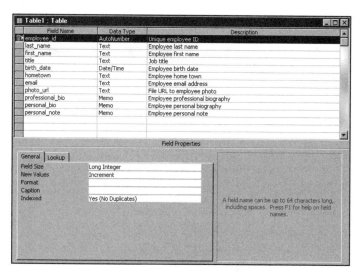

FIGURE 3.7   *Selecting the employee_id field as the primary key.*

Finally, click the Save toolbar button (a button with a disk centered on its face) to save the table definition.

A dialog box will appear prompting for the name of the table definition (see Figure 3.8). Type **Employees** and click OK to save the table definition. Close the Design View window of the Employees table and you will see an icon representing the Employees table object in the Database Manager window.

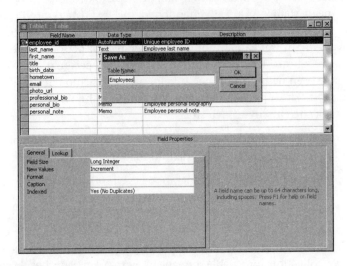

FIGURE 3.8   *You can specify the name of the new table in this dialog box.*

Go ahead and repeat this process for the Favorites table (see Figure 3.9).

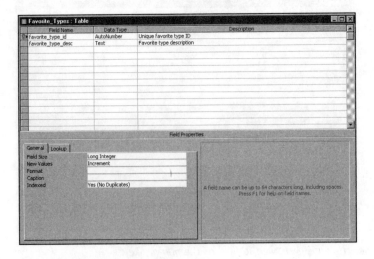

FIGURE 3.9   *The definition for the Favorites table.*

And the Skills table (see Figure 3.10).

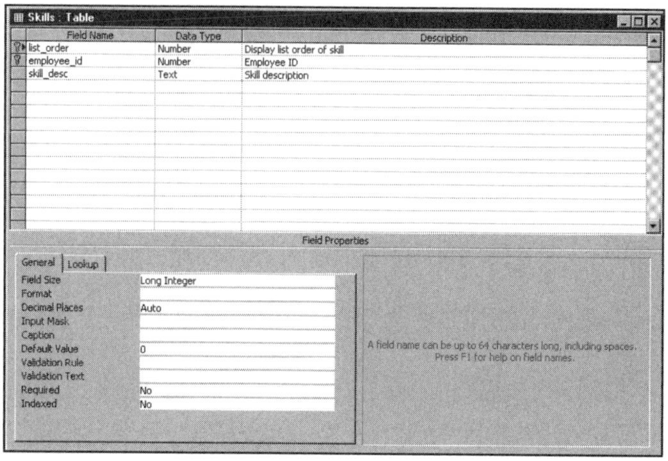

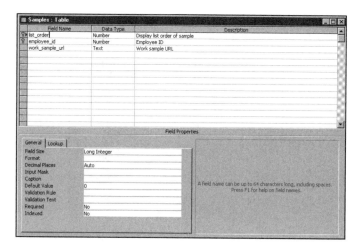

FIGURE 3.10   *The definition for the Skills table.*

And finally, the Samples table (see Figure 3.11).

FIGURE 3.11   *The definition for the Samples table.*

Next, you establish referential integrity between the tables that were just added to the database. With only the Database Manager window open, click the Relationships toolbar button (the depressed button in Figure 3.12). A dialog box appears prompting for a list of table and/or query objects that should be made available in the Relationships window (visible in the background).

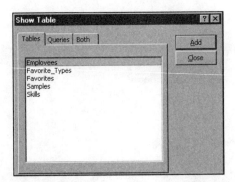

FIGURE 3.12   *You can specify which tables to define relationships for in this dialog box.*

Select all five tables and click the Add button to display the table definitions in the Relationships window. Click the Close button to remove the dialog box.

Arrange the tables in the relationship window so that the Employees table is in the center. To establish a relationship between the Employees table and the Favorites table, click and drag the employee_id (primary key) field in the Employees table over the employee_id (foreign key) field in the Favorites table and then release. A dialog box appears displaying the relationship between the Employees and Favorites tables (One-to-Many) and provides a check box that, if set, will enforce referential integrity between the two tables (see Figure 3.13).

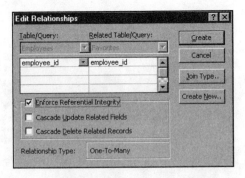

FIGURE 3.13   *You can define the relationship between two tables in this dialog box.*

Set the check box and click the Create button to establish referential integrity between the two tables.

A line connecting the two tables will appear graphically representing the association between Employees records and Favorites records. Note the "infinity" symbol on the Favorites end of the association connector and the "one" symbol on the Employees end. This notation indicates the fact that for every unique record in the Employees table, there may exist zero, one, or many associated records in the Favorites table. In other words, an employee may have multiple favorites associated with him or her.

Repeat this process for the remaining tables to establish referential integrity across the entire employee database as illustrated in Figure 3.14.

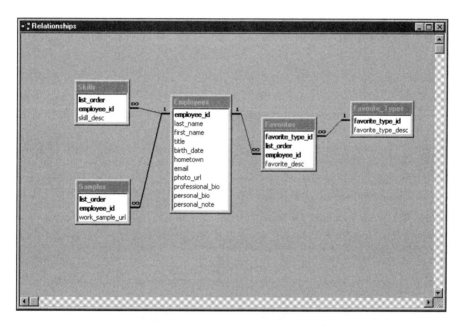

FIGURE 3.14   *Here are the table relationships for the employee database.*

Save these additions to the database design and close the Relationships window.

The final step in implementing the employee database is to insert some sample data into the tables that have just been defined. The simplest way to do this is to double-click a table object in the Database Manager window, which causes the selected table object to open in data-entry mode. At that point, you can directly add, modify, and delete data within the table.

Start with the Employees table by double-clicking its icon in the Database Manager window. The Employees table opens in data-entry mode with no fields currently defined. Add one record as follows:

- last_name: Groch
- first_name: Matthew
- email: mgroch@2-mc.com
- birth_date: 6/18/1976
- title: Project Manager
- photo_url: C:\Inetpub\wwwroot\employee\dataEntryToolImages\empPhotos\ mgroch.jpg
- hometown: Chicago, IL
- professional_bio: A smart guy
- personal_bio: A nice guy
- personal_note: Hello world!

The Employees table should look similar to Figure 3.15.

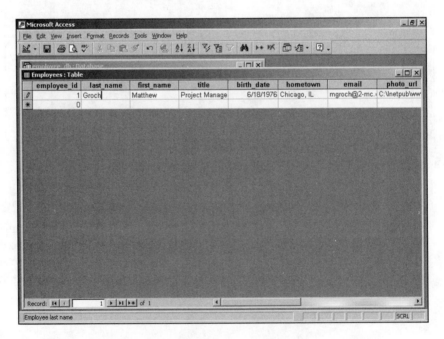

FIGURE 3.15 *This is the data entry view of the Employees table.*

Now add one more record to the Employees table:

- last_name: Imran
- first_name: Mohamed
- email: imohamed@2-mc.com
- birth_date: 10/31/1974
- title: Director of Operations
- photo_url: C:\Inetpub\wwwroot\employee\dataEntryToolImages\empPhotos\ imohamed.jpg
- hometown: Long_Grove
- professional_bio: A smarter guy
- personal_bio: A nicer guy
- personal_note: Goodbye, cruel world!

Okay, close the Employees table. Repeat this process to add sample data to the Favorite_Types, Favorites, Skills, and Samples tables. For example, the Favorite_Types table should have only three records: one for the "movies" favorite type, one for the "books" favorite type, and one for the "bands" favorite type. And that's it! You now have a fully implemented employee database residing in Microsoft Access that is ready for the application development phase of the employee Web site.

Accessing the Data (SQL 101)

Of course, a critical component of the application development of the employee Web site involves the actual retrieval of data from the employee database. Data retrieval is nearly always performed through the execution of SQL queries.

SQL (usually pronounced like the word *sequel*), or Structured Query Language, is a specification for retrieving and modifying data stored within relational databases. Pretty much every commercial relational database management system implements some flavor of the ANSI SQL 92 version of the specification.

In the context of the employee Web site, you construct a set of SQL queries that retrieves the sample data that has been inserted into the employee database to complete this example.

Retrieval of data using SQL is performed through the submission of a SELECT statement to the database. While the syntax for the SELECT statement allows data queries to become quite complicated, the queries in this example will remain relatively simple in accordance with the complexity level of the employee database.

The general form of a simple SELECT statement is as follows:

```
SELECT
{field names}
FROM {table names}
{WHERE {filter criteria}}
{ORDER BY {field names} {DESC}}
```

Basically, this type of SQL command says to the database, "Give me all the values from fields named X, Y, and Z that exist in tables named A and B where the values in field X conform to some criteria, the values in field Y conform to some criteria, and the values in field Z conform to some criteria. Also, sort the records you give me by the values in field Z."

Practical examples will illustrate the point. The first SELECT statement to construct obtains the list of employees in the database in alphabetic order.

```
SELECT
*
FROM
Employees
ORDER BY last_name,first_name
```

First, notice the asterisk in lieu of a list of field names. The asterisk is a symbol that indicates that the database should return values for *all* the fields in each record returned from the table. Because you want to obtain all the information for each employee, you can use this nice shortcut in conjunction with the explicit nonuse of the WHERE filter clause. (That is, you want *all* employee records.) Next, notice how the ORDER BY clause contains two field names. This is telling the database that the set of records returned should be ordered (first by last name, and then by first name).

In Access, you can enter SQL queries and execute them directly against the database. To execute the preceding SQL query, click the Queries menu item on the left side of the Database Manager window.

As Figure 3.16 illustrates, the Database Manager window presents two ways to create queries. Double-click the first right-side item to begin entering your first SQL statement. By default, Access displays a Query-Builder window that you can use to create SQL statements in a tabular fashion. The first thing that happens is that Access prompts you for a list of tables you will use to build a new query. Because you will be using SQL to build your queries, go ahead and close this window without selecting any of the tables in the employee database.

To create a query as a SQL statement, click the first button on the main Access toolbar (a button with the letters *SQL* on the face beside a down arrow). This is a toggle button that automatically translates a query from its design (tabular) view to its SQL view. (See Figure 3.17.)

FIGURE 3.16   *Queries menu options in the Database Manager window.*

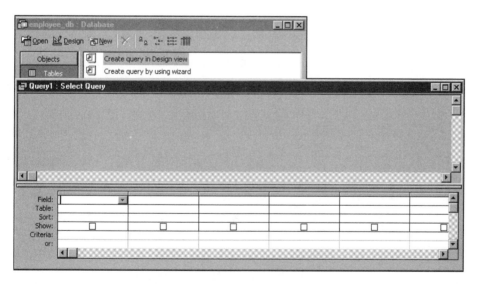

FIGURE 3.17   *This is the Design View window for building queries in Access.*

As illustrated in Figure 3.18, enter the sample SQL statement that retrieves all information about all employees into the SQL View window. Then, to execute the query, click the Run button on the main Access toolbar (a button with a red exclamation point on its face). The view window changes once more, this time into a datasheet view that displays the results of the query you just entered.

You can use this mechanism within Access to design, build, and test the rest of your SQL queries for the employees Web site (see Figure 3.19).

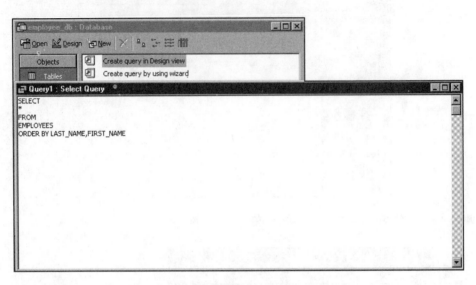

FIGURE 3.18   *This is the SQL View window for building queries in Access.*

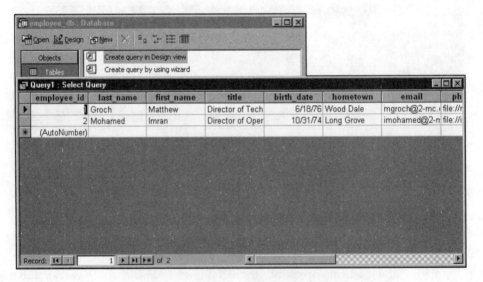

FIGURE 3.19   *This is the Datasheet View window for queries built in Access.*

In the context of the employee Web site, now suppose that a representative from Big International Company is viewing a list of the employees on the Web site's main page and wants to learn more about the second employee on the list. All the information pertaining to that particular employee needs to be retrieved from the database for display as the representative browses the employee-specific pages.

First, the employee's top-three favorite movies, books, and bands display; assuming that in the Favorite_Types table, the movies type has an ID of 1, the books type has an ID of 2, and the bands type has an ID of 3:

For movies:

```
SELECT favorite_desc FROM Favorites WHERE employee_id = 2 AND
favorite_type_id = 1 AND list_order <= 3 ORDER BY list_order
```

For books:

```
SELECT favorite_desc FROM Favorites WHERE employee_id = 2 AND
favorite_type_id = 2 AND list_order <= 3 ORDER BY list_order
```

And for bands:

```
SELECT favorite_desc FROM Favorites WHERE employee_id = 3 AND
favorite_type_id = 3 AND list_order <= 3 ORDER BY list_order
```

Second, the employee's skill set:

```
SELECT skill_desc FROM Skills WHERE employee_id = 2 AND list_order <= 10
ORDER BY list_order
```

And finally, the employee's links to work samples:

```
SELECT work_sample_url FROM Samples WHERE employee_id = 2 ORDER BY
list_order
```

At last, you are finished. You now have a fully implemented employee database populated with data; and even more importantly, you have a mechanism through which you can retrieve that information as necessary. With a little scripting work, you will be ready to start putting the whole employee Web site together with Generator!

Summary

In this chapter, you explored the following topics:

- **Database 101.** A database is a container of data organized as a collection of tables, records, and fields. Together with server-side scripting and Structured Query Language (SQL), you can define and manipulate data specific to your requirements, which is an ideal way to supply a data source to Generator.

- **Server-side scripting 101.** Server-side scripting languages, such as ASP (Active Server Pages), PHP, ColdFusion, JSP (Java Server Pages), and Tcl, are robust programming scripting languages that perform commands on the Web server and return as results to the browser. They enable you to access a database, respond to user input, work with an OS file system, and give you the ability to create dynamic pages.

- **The employee database.** The employee database was created using Microsoft Access. Using the ideas and elements identified during the brainstorming sessions and storyboards as the data elements, the database was constructed as a relational set of tables.

- **SQL.** Sometimes known as SEQUEL (For Structured English QUEry Language), SQL is the standard interface language for database-management systems, such as Microsoft Access. SQL is constructed as a series of statements that define, manipulate, and sort data in a database. It also provides certain levels of database security,

- **Generator data source.** A data source in Generator is a collection of static values in a text file, a URL, or a Java class. As long as any of these data sources provide information in a recognizable comma-delimited format, Generator can work with them.

The database is the heart and soul of dynamic site development. The concepts and skills learned in this chapter can be easily adapted to fit your online dynamic site development projects as well. The database management system not only holds your project data, but also organizes and enables you to manage the data as well. This is key in supplying data sources to Generator for processing Flash.

Most DBA books and classes will have you believe that organizing information in a database system is a high-level project filled with all the challenges of astrophysics and postmodern philosophy. Don't be intimidated. If you have ever maintained an address book in your life, you're well on your way to setting up a database for offline Generator development. Every employee has a first name, last name, job function, and so on. Microsoft Access allows for quick-and-easy database creation and accomplishes a good deal of the hard work for you, thanks to SQL.

This chapter introduced you to the world of database design and its implementation. You started by taking a look at the internal core of all database systems. With your understating of database terminology and how they work, you then looked at the available choices in database systems. Finally, using Microsoft Access, you constructed the database that will be used in the mock employee site. With this key element in place, the next chapter shows you how to construct the templates that use Generator objects and data sources from the database. In Chapter 5, "The Data-Entry Tool," you construct the data-entry tool for entering and modifying content in the database. Chapter 6, "Final Production: Putting All the Pieces Together," pulls these three key elements (the database, the template, and the data-entry tool) together. This final production shows you how all these three key elements work in unison for Generator processing and final site development.

CHAPTER 4

Building the Templates

This chapter focuses on building the templates, the fourth in a six-step workflow process using offline Generator. In particular, this chapter covers the following topics:

- Flash movie and template design basics
- File optimization
- Designing templates using standard practices
- Introduction to the Generator objects
- Utilizing dynamic content in the template design
- Building the employee template pages

You now have the information regarding the design and storyboards and have started the database. Now it is time to start building the templates. This chapter takes you through the initial processes of establishing a strong foundation for beginning templates, the standards, and the practices that apply to developing/designing templates, the use of Generator objects, and ultimately to a well-rounded and thought-out template design ready for publishing.

Templates and the Overall Design

Most designers/developers of Web content have probably cranked out templates for HTML documents and image systems. This chapter is still instructive, however, because Generator templates take into play various amounts of depth and motion not generally found with static design.

With regard to initial design, a Generator template does not differ from a normal Flash file. In fact, it helps to design as you normally would by bringing in all elements of the design, setting up scenes and keyframes based on the storyboards, establishing a frame rate, and so on. With Adobe Photoshop, Adobe Illustrator, and Macromedia Freehand, layers play an important role in establishing depth; the same goes for Flash. The main difference is that after the design is laid out and the flow of the movie has been established, a certain deconstruction method comes into play when the file would otherwise be finished. In return, turning your gold into lead while enabling you to achieve more of what you set out to do at a much faster pace.

The discussion starts by focusing on the basics of production. Basics here cover only the root elements of the employee site. We establish the actual movie structure from the storyboards as we move along through the chapter. For now, however, it is time to just start a new Flash file.

The storyboards show the dimensions and frame rate of the intended movies, and these elements are all we need to begin. Note that these may or may not be to your liking or need, so feel free to take the initiative to alter your movies as you see fit and to what feels the most comfortable to you while working through this chapter.

After choosing to start a new file, the first thing you do is set the dimensions and the frame rate. The frame rate of 30 frames per second (fps) was established for the employee profile site because it will run live over an intranet and is intended to have decently smooth animation. The dimensions of the movies were established because of the dominant monitor resolution (800×600) that most of the employees will be viewing the profiles on.

To set the frame rate and the dimensions of a new movie, go to the Applications menu and click Modify. Then click Movie. With the Movie Properties panel open, enter the values from the storyboards or whatever your design may call for. If you plan to use this setting for most of the movies you develop, you can select to save it as the default. After you have done this, anytime you elect to create a new movie, it will open with these settings.

After the base for the movies has been established, set your sites on the overall picture. A basic understanding of elements that make up the Flash content and structure is the concern.

Keep in mind that any design as well as tweening/animation is completely up to you, your style, and your level of Flash. The rest of the chapter should help you determine how and why you should make your design come alive. Even though this is not a design book in the traditional sense, you can find great tips and tricks throughout this and the other chapters. Take them as a starting point, but remember to always think creatively and look forward (not relying on past progression) when designing for and with technology.

Dynamic Elements Versus Static Elements

Before beginning to work with templates, consider the two main elements discussed earlier during the planning stage: dynamic and static elements. Because either may be constructed of movie clips, smart clips, text fields, or buttons, their differences are sometimes indistinguishable. Sometimes dynamic areas are embedded in static elements, such as a text box in a movie clip; such is the case for the employee photo (see "Working with Generator Objects" later in this chapter). Working with both elements can create some confusion, especially if you are asked to clean up some bugs in someone else's file. Knowing the differences between the two before production will definitely ease the workflow stress.

Not to confuse anyone: Static elements in a template are not limited to just sitting still or remaining stagnant—which, by the way, is the beauty of Flash as a tool. Just imagine that there is a movie clip made up of various lines constantly moving in the background. Does it change color when certain user interactions are recorded? Does it change to bubbles? If it does, most likely it is a dynamic element, not static. The real question is will it be dynamically altered with the use of Generator? If the answer is no, you have your answer. Anything that is or will not be produced using Generator is a static element. Anything that will be altered with Generator is considered dynamic.

Dynamic elements for Generator are altered based on information passed to your template. They can either be variables or Generator objects. We all know that we can create dynamic elements within Flash by itself; for the Generator level, however, creating dynamic elements means that certain instances and text fields will be altered by the use of Generator objects and variables.

note

Static Versus Dynamic. Think of static elements as items that once designed, laid out, and possibly tweened (animated), will not change based on information passed to the template. They are as you designed them; nothing will be different about them the next time you load/generate the movie.

Dynamic elements are very similar. You design them, lay them out, and animate them. When the movie is generated, however, those items are expected to alter their content in some way.

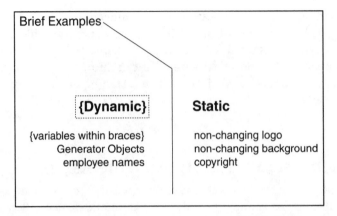

Figure 4.1   *Brief examples of both dynamic and static elements pertaining to the mock employee site. Note that the dynamic elements contain curly braces surrounding the variables.*

With regard to dynamic elements pertaining to Generator and most importantly the employee templates, most of the dynamic elements within the employee site will be text elements. In fact, the only item that isn't text is the employee photo, which is a Generator JPG object within a movie clip. What is important about both the text and the photo is that they will require a special format for Generator to recognize as being dynamic. Don't worry, however; it is not something for which you need to go back to school.

For Generator to accept variables for dynamic content, the name needs to be encompassed between a beginning curly brace and an ending curly brace, as follows:

```
{thisIsAVariableForGenerator}
```

If the curly braces are not present, Generator will not recognize your variables and it is more than likely you will see exactly what you typed (if you typed it as a text item) when you try to preview your movie. This is not the desired effect. What this really means is that what you thought was a dynamic variable that would be replaced by text from your database or text file will display as a static element.

Simply put, static elements are not produced with Generator, dynamic elements are.

Generator Help. For more information regarding variables within Generator, refer to the Generator Help section under "Generator Basics: Creating and Using Variables."

Standards and Practices

Now that you have a basic understanding of the two main elements that comprise a template, you can focus on some of the fundamentals that make up those elements. In addition, as you prepare the templates for the employee site, you also should be familiar with a few common practices and standards that have surfaced while developing within Flash.

This section also covers various uses of ActionScript, Flash's object-oriented programming language. Note, however, that the intent of covering ActionScript (within this book) is not to explain in-depth advanced scripting or programming for Flash.

> **note**
>
> **ActionScript Info.** If you want to become more involved with Flash ActionScripting, you can visit numerous resources online and off. A couple of good Web sites are FlashKit (**www.flashkit.com**), which has tutorials for beginners and experts, along with downloadable source files; and Praystation (**www.praystation.com**), which has examples of advanced interactivity Action-Scripting; and Actionscript.com (**www.actionscript.com**), which has fairly regular updates and in-depth examples of ActionScripting (especially with regard to making the transition from Flash 4 to Flash 5). All three are excellent choices to help guide new and old users alike. Check out Appendix B, "Resources," for more Flash resources!

Edit in Place

Before delving into standards and practices, this discussion turns to the designer's best friend: the Edit in Place function.

Flash is most likely responsible for the number of traditional designers working on Web development because Flash enables WYSIWYG (what you see is what you get) development and most designers are extremely visual. What makes Flash even more attractive is its capability to see layer after layer beneath the initial surface of the Flash work area while still allowing the surrounding elements to remain visible (but grayed back a bit).

Because most design-oriented programs such as Freehand, Illustrator, and Photoshop allow layering, most designers are used to the depth. Flash offers greater depth, allowing its timeline and movie clip's separate timelines to work in conjunction with its layering system as well.

To work more efficiently, the Edit in Place function is a must. By using Edit in Place with an object you would like to alter, instead of looking through the library and having to edit without any context to the rest of the movie, you can achieve better results with placement of objects containing multiple objects and timelines. Also, when choosing to edit in place, a breadcrumb type of navigation appears in the upper-left corner of the top of the stage. This program functionality will ease the editing of elements as you work through the employee site.

Consider this example. You need to edit the rollover state of one of your buttons, but you also need to see how it will look with the rest of the site (mainly to see whether it covers anything up or whether it is not lining up with the correct element on the main timeline). When faced with such a scenario, you can reach the Edit in Place function as follows:

1. Select the button in question.

2. Right-click (PC) or Ctrl-click (MAC).

3. Select Edit in Place from the drop-down menu.

As you can see, using Edit in Place can be a life saver, especially if you have a great deal of items in your library and need to design and develop while keeping an eye on your surroundings.

Scenes

When creating any Flash file, you must also create and set up the scenes. They may or may not be needed, depending on the size and content of the project, but they are still more than worthy. Not only do they help to separate content, but they also enable you to solve loading issues. Assume, for instance, that you have a total of four scenes. The first is a loader, the second holds all main content, the third contains elements for loading and unloading external movie clips, and the fourth contains elements for help (see Figure 4.2).

Figure 4.2   *Flash's Scene panel.*

Movies generally play scenes from top to bottom, if there is no ActionScript based on time intervals or a user interaction pointing to scenes in no specific play order. The example scenes in Figure 4.2 could be set up to play from Intro to Main Nav, stop, wait for a

note

Unstreaming. Movie clips do not stream.

selection from the navigation, and then based on that selection could jump to the Load/Unload Clips, pause, and then load an external movie clip or point to the Help scene.

Having the scenes set up this way allows for the latter three to load behind the first. By the time the user has finished adjusting his or her new surroundings, the other scenes will be loaded. Setting up a smart clip or movie clip that would contain a keyframe of each item would work nicely. Remember, however, that neither will show until they're completely loaded. Therefore, scenes are your best bet.

To establish a good working base for templates, you may find it easiest to begin by setting up separate blank movies and scenes according to what is required in the schematics, storyboards, and wireframes. The storyboards for the employee site show that there are really only two movies, the main movie (with main navigation), and the employee movie (template for each employee). Because the main movie won't be dynamic, you do not need to construct it as a template. It is the base movie, however, and you should set it up to accommodate the `loadMovie` command (mentioned later in this chapter) to further smooth the transitions to and from the employee pages.

Again, referring to the flowchart and the storyboards, note that the architecture shows only two movies. Also shown, each movie has specific elements contained only in its respective movie and scenes. One movie (main) is to contain the navigation of the employees and the base elements that will not need to be replicated in the employee templates, but will obviously need to contain space for the templates to load and unload from (acting as a docking bay). Then there is the second movie (the employee Generator template) that will contain all relevant information about specific employees.

The concept of using only one movie for the employees themselves is simple. To do so, follow these steps:

1. Design a template that can be updated dynamically using Generator.

2. Generate the employee-specific information for every employee listed.

3. Load them into the shell movie that contains information that does not change often to create a seamless electronic experience.

Take a look at the main movie's scenes. To open the Scene panel (Mac and PC), go to the Application menu and select Windows/Panels/Scene. (See Figure 4.3.)

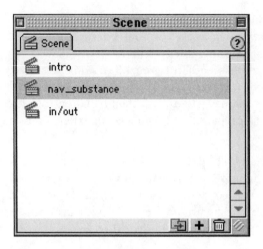

FIGURE 4.3   *The main movies scenes set up within the Scene panel.*

To add additional scenes, click the plus sign (+) icon located on the lower-right of the panel, until three new scenes are added. Select each scene in order by double-clicking the title, and label them with the exact name or an abbreviation that can easily be understood; you will have to reference them later.

While you're at it, go ahead and set the following scenes for the employee template, following the example set earlier:

- Default
- Favorites
- Professional Biography
- Personal Biography
- Skills and Samples
- In Their Own words

One last bit on the advantage of using scenes to separate key areas of content is the reduction of blank keyframes throughout the entire movie (including the other scenes). This saves file space and reduces the amount of layers in a given scene's timeline.

Beware of Size. For the most part, the simple rule of creating movies that will load into another movie is incredibly important. If the size is off, items in the loaded movie may not display in their correct positions.

Having the scenes set up in the beginning is not a firm rule, but it will ease the flow of progress and help create a clearer understanding of how the templates or Flash files are organized.

Layers

You have set up the scenes for the templates; what now? Well, the next step for further establishment of a base for Flash files is the set up of layers. No one should be a stranger to layers; developers use them with DHTML, and designers use them with graphics programs. They are key when organizing elements either in Photoshop, Freehand, or Fireworks. Why would Flash differ? It does not. Only a few uses are not present when working with other programs.

> **note**
>
> **Switching Scenes.** You can visually switch between scenes by clicking the appropriately named title in the Scene panel. While working with scenes, therefore, it is a good idea to keep the panel open. You can keep it on the desktop by itself or drag its tab to one of the other panels and drop it in. Because there is no keyboard shortcut, this will make it available to you anytime during your session in Flash. You can save your panel layout for future use as well by selecting Window/Save Panel Layout.

With layers come depth, especially when tweening/animating. This notion of depth is accentuated by the layer order. Layers are viewed from top to bottom, so special attention should be paid to the design and interactivity of the proposed design. What this means is that if you have layers titled "menu shadow" and "menu," more than likely "menu" should be listed above "menu shadow" (as far as layer positioning on the timeline is concerned). The layer order (from top to bottom or bottom to top) should reflect the intended load/stream order as well.

To specify the load order (Mac and PC), go to the Application menu and select File/Publish Settings.

In the Publish Settings panel, click the Flash tab. The very first item listed is the Load Order drop-down menu. For the purposes of the mock site templates, select Bottom. (See Figure 4.4.) The reason is purely preferential because you can position the layers in any order you want. In most cases, however, the template has been designed with some type of depth in mind, and certain elements may overlap others. By loading from the bottom, the template loads base elements first and builds on them, further accentuating the pseudo depth already acquired.

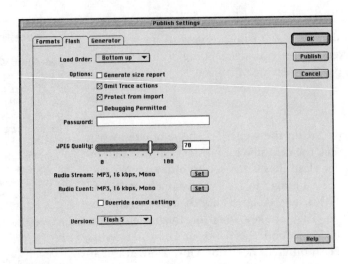

FIGURE 4.4   *The Publish Settings panel.*

When first importing elements from the final design into Flash, you may find it easiest to define layers for each of the elements that you know will be tweened/animated, static, dynamic, and so forth. The more you have separated elements on their own layers, the easier and faster the template transition process will be. Also, this will help eliminate the deletion and repositioning of key elements, especially if you lock all layers you are not currently working on.

With these reasons tucked under your hat, go ahead and add a layer (the guide layer). (See Figure 4.5.)

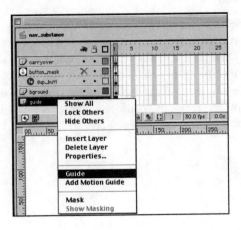

FIGURE 4.5   *The Layer drop-down menu.*

To set up a new layer to be used as a guide (Mac and PC), follow these steps:

1. Click the plus sign icon located at the bottom left of the timeline underneath the layer titles.

2. Name it **guide** and drag it all the way to the bottom of the timeline.

3. Double-click the icon on the right of the label name so that the Layer Property panel opens.

4. Select guide and click OK.

Alternatively, in the application menu, select Insert/Layer.

All elements that are to remain visible from the main movie should be copied and placed into the new guide layer. This way the coordination of design and animation can be implemented with ease because you can see what the movie will look like while you are still designing (as if it were loaded). Thus, no guesswork is at hand.

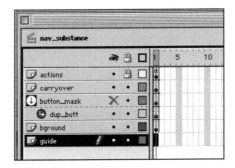

FIGURE 4.6   *The added guide layer. Note its position beneath the other layers.*

After you have set up the guide layer on the first screen, copy and paste the same layer into each of the other scenes. Make sure to keep it at the bottom of your layer order so that nothing is hidden. When each scene has its guide layer set up, you are ready to roll.

To copy and paste layers (Mac and PC), follow these steps:

1. In the Application menu, select Edit/Copy Frames.

2. Select the appropriate scene, using the Scene Panel or the Scene icon in the upper-right of the Application window.

note

Storyboards. Based on the storyboards from Chapter 2, "Designing Beyond Look and Feel," the guide layer should be re-created for each scene of the template.

3. Either select a keyframe on an empty layer or create a new layer to paste your frames into.

4. Choose Edit/Paste Frames.

Be sure not to get "layer happy." Too many layers can cause confusion and a larger file size. It is always good practice to keep size issues in mind (and thereby keep your co-workers from cursing your development habits).

Masks

Ever wished that something would disappear just for a little while? Just as designers are used to elemental layers in their favorite graphics software, it is a sure bet that they are just as familiar with masks.

Mask layers are generally used throughout Flash production and development to hide portions of or show specific portions of text, movie clips, symbols, Generator objects, and even entire stage areas. For the purposes of the example templates, you will be masking the dynamic text portions of the employee scenes. Obviously, the single text fields won't need this method applied, but the scenes containing the biographies and other possibly lengthy text fields will.

By using the mask layer, you can hide any portion of text considered to be out-of-area (*out-of-area text* is any overflow not intended to be seen outside of its designed space, but present at a given point). Suppose, for instance, that you have four paragraphs of text that will be included when the templates are processed, but there is space allocated to the design for only one paragraph. With the use of buttons to control the scrolling and a Mask layer to hide the remaining text, you can resolve this issue.

The content for the mask layer can be a grouped symbol or a straight vector shape. By making it a symbol all its own, however, it can be reused and its shape transformed to fit other mask layers throughout the movie with no added file size. You can even use a symbol already present in the library (such as a background element used for color). Basically, you can use any solid, filled, or static element as a mask.

Let's go through the motions of setting the mask up using gibberish text as a placeholder.

The simple task of creating a new layer (discussed previously) and positioning it directly over the layer the mask will be applied to is the first step. The second involves a minor change to the layer's properties. While the new layer is selected as editable, open the

note

Check Out the Source Files. Just so you know, the navigation for the employees in the main movie uses a mask to hide the excess names. For a more detailed understanding, explore the source files on the CD-ROM. These will shed quite a bit of light.

Layer Properties panel by double-clicking the icon to the left of the new layer's title. From the list that displays, select Mask. Click OK. The layer is now set as a mask. Changing the layer's properties from within the Layer Properties panel sets up only that particular layer as a mask. Therefore, by setting up your masks this way, you will again have to open the Layer Properties panel and change settings, this time for the layer to be masked. (See Figure 4.7.)

FIGURE 4.7   *Setting up a mask layer in the Layer Properties panel.*

To save time making masked layers (basically killing two birds with one stone), press Ctrl+click (Mac) or right-click (PC) the layer that you intend to make a mask. The drop-down menu appears. After you have selected Mask, both layers become locked and the layer directly beneath the new mask layer is positioned to the right, signifying its association with the mask. (See Figure 4.8.)

In some circumstances, you may need to adjust the shape of your mask. Just click the padlock icon to the right of the layer's name and you're ready to go. The main thing to keep in mind when sizing masks is the area you want to display. If it is off just a hair, some unwanted elements could appear and disrupt the design.

note

Additional Layers. Adding an additional layer on top of the mask layer is a good idea if there are boundaries for text in the design. A layer added beneath the last layer being masked can serve as a background layer. This all depends on how the movie/site is designed and on personal taste.

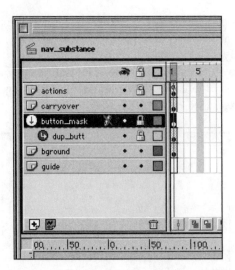

FIGURE 4.8   *The locked mask and masked layers. Note their relationship to each other with the arrow icons.*

If the text field is set up within a movie clip all its own, you can scroll it by using ActionScript to control either the X or Y position properties of the text movie clip (depending on whether you want it to move horizontally or vertically and whether it has been given a variable to call when a user response is recorded). The navigation for the employees in the main movie uses the vertical method.

Anyway, masks serve a definite purpose when developing with Flash (especially with content-heavy sites). They are highly recommended. Besides, they clean up your design.

Actions Layer

Another important layer a template should never be without is the ever-popular actions layer. A staple of production, it enables you to quickly refer to label names. The actions layer should contain all relevant ActionScripting for that particular scene in the timeline. Variables for dynamic content, scripts for interactivity, and comments are its usual inhabitants.

The actions layer is a must have. It will serve as the horizontal organizer for the entire movie/template. Just as you use the layer titles to make adjustments to key elements residing on those layers, you use the actions layer to locate keyframes, labels, and pivotal ActionScripts (all of which are key elements that control the movie).

For the most part, the actions layer is positioned at the very top of the list in the layer section on the timeline. Again, this is for ease of access and organization. You also may position it at the bottom of the list, depending on the load order specified (see the section titled "Layers" earlier in this chapter). (See Figure 4.9.)

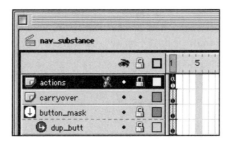

FIGURE 4.9   *Note the position of the actions layer in the timeline. Normally, it should be placed either above all other layers or below all other layers (depending on the load order specified).*

What good is an actions layer without actions?

Because the features of ActionScript merit a whole other book on their own, this book covers only these elements of the ActionScript language that were actually used to build the employee profile site. Note also that the purpose for listing these uses of ActionScript is not to explain every possible usage. Instead, a brief explanation of how ActionScript was used will aid your progress through this book and future Flash endeavors.

Before actually putting actions to work, take the time to finish importing all your design elements from either Illustrator or Freehand (whichever you are using) and begin setting up your final animation and scene settings. Continue with this section only when you are in a comfortable position with the timing and spacing of elements in the timeline. Take a look back at the storyboards from Chapter 2 to refresh your memory as well.

It is now time to consider one of the major action layers within the movie: the duplication action layer (see "duplicateMovieClip" section later in this chapter.)

The following list shows how the layer is set up for the duplication action layer; there are four keyframes:

- The first will contain ActionScript to load the total number of employees/buttons and the links that each button will need to load the movie specific to each employee.
- The second keyframe will be blank so that the first set of variables has time to load into the main movie before the duplication process begins.
- The third keyframe will contain the actual duplication script
- The fourth keyframe will contain script that will load the employee names into place (after the buttons have been duplicated).

As you can see, the actions layer does not look like much. Its real importance is its organization. Each keyframe and its set of actions will more than likely play a huge part in the load time, playback, and functionality of the movie. Knowing how your actions layer is set up will enable you to easily make alterations to specific areas of code.

Consider the duplications actions layer just discussed. Suppose that you want to change the name of the text file that contains your employee names. After saving the text file with a different name, you need to change it in the Flash file as well. Remembering that your employee names are loaded in the fourth frame on your ActionScript layer, you can quickly jump right in and make your adjustment, regenerate your movie, and then you're all set. If you give your keyframes titles, you can easily see the keyframe by its relative name (and can therefore browse your movie's scripts even faster).

You should set each of your action layers so that you or your team members can implement changes without having a specific designer or developer present. Workflow depends on organization, and action layers should reflect your workflow.

Instance-Naming Conventions

This section discusses instance names that reference various movie clips throughout both the main movie and the employee template. Therefore, it is first necessary to understand what they are and why they are so named. If you are unfamiliar with instance naming, read on. (You also should browse the Flash Help file.)

An *instance* is roughly a name given to a movie clip for reference by ActionScript. You also can consider the name to be a variable of some sort. When you have interaction between movie clips with the with statement (see the sections "with This or That" and "Working with Generator Objects" later in this chapter) or want to use

ActionScript to `getProperties` of certain movie clips for any reason, those movie clips need a reference name. Without some way of referencing your clips, virtually nothing could be done with them as far as ActionScript goes.

Following is a possible instance-naming convention:

> **note**
>
> **Library and Instance Names.** The most common instance names are always similar to the actual library item name.

- If the movie clip is named dup, the instance could be dup.

- If the movie clip is named wonderfulheadhurt, the instance could be named headhurt.

The point of a naming convention with instances is to keep things short and similar so that no floundering happens and guesswork is minimal. Remember that you will be referencing these names in your scripts. Keep them simple.

To give a movie clip an instance name, follow these steps:

1. Select a movie clip that you will be referencing.

2. Do one of the following two things:

   - Select the Instance panel on the desktop.

   - Go to Modify: Instance in the Application menu.

3. With the Instance panel displayed, type the name. Voilà, you're done.

duplicateMovieClip (the Main Navigation)

One of the standards we have been following with our own work, almost like religion, is the use of the "duplicate movie" ActionScript element. This little bit of wondercode saves the day every time. Just a fair warning; this section does cover ActionScript and does get a bit "techie." It is mainly here to help explain the logic behind the duplication method. Although it would be to your advantage to understand as much as possible about its functionality, we won't be upset if you just copy and paste from the original source file; in fact, it's encouraged.

Do you need to dynamically create a scrolling list without Generator? What if the scrolling list has to contain more than 500 buttons? With rollovers? Well, get ready, you are going to save an unbelievable amount of file size.

Here is the scoop: You are going to have 50 names for the employee list. If you were to make each a button in Flash, the file size would probably scream out of control and turn into a lead weight. Using the `duplicateMovieClip` with the navigation will make things much easier by enabling you to reuse the same button for each of the employee names and by using a text file to load the variables that will populate the text fields. Also, the variables for up to 50 names can load a Flash movie with lots of extra K and bloat the file size (yet another good reason for the text file variables).

With the basic understanding of the need to create a dynamic text file navigation out of the way, it is time to go over the actual structure of such a widget. Following are the elements of the Duplication Scroller:

- **wholeroller.** The movie clip that will contain every element listed below. Everything within the scrolling navigation can be dragged and dropped without altering the existing code if it is built with mobility in mind; such is the reason for the wholeroller movie clip.

- **rollers.** The movie clip that will contain the navigation, ActionScript for the duplication and load variables.

- **dup.** The movie clip that will be duplicated and hold the employee names and loadMovie (see "loadMovie" later in this chapter) ActionScript.

- The (invisible) button. The text field.

- **control.** The movie clip that contains the actions for the scrollers.

Notice that this type of navigation entails multiple movie clips. Working with instances quickly comes into play when dealing with such hierarchy. The best way to understand such organization is to build it, or look at someone else's code (which you can do by looking through the source files on the accompanying CD). You can always take the easy road and drag the entire wholemovieclip out of the CD library and into your own movie for deconstruction.

Suppose that you have the main movie open and have the scroller selected. This is an Edit in Place type of moment. Therefore while the scroller is selected, Edit in Place until you reach the roller level. (Edit in Place twice—once on the wholeroller movie clip, and once again on the rollers movie clip.)

Before delving further into the actions, open the Actions panel by following these steps:

1. Select either the keyframe, movie clip, or button for which you will be adding or editing the actions.

2. Follow the same method used to display the drop-down menu as Edit in Place. (That is, right-click [PC] or Ctrl-click [MAC] on the item [frame or symbol] and select Actions).

Now, take a look at the code that actually makes the buttons.

```
while (n < total) {
    n = (n)+1;
    bn = "dup" + n;
    duplicateMovieClip ("dup", bn, n);
    setProperty (bn, _y, (getProperty(bn, _y))+n*(getProperty(bn,
_height)));
    set (bn add ":n", n);
}
_root:dupH = _parent.roller.dup._height*total;
```

The entire duplication process takes place in the third frame. The infamous duplicateMovieClip finally rears its wonderful-head (hurt). It is easiest to understand this section with the important lines broken down. (See Figure 4.10.)

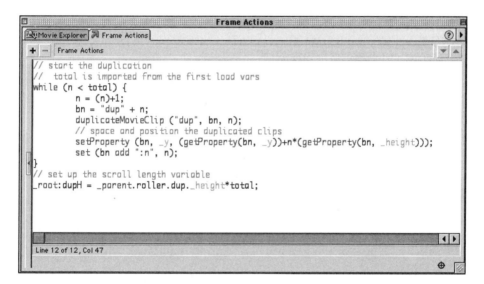

FIGURE 4.10 *The actions for the duplication method.*

The basic functions of the preceding code is to keep duplicating the original movie until the total variable is met, all while positioning each duplicate beneath the last, creating a long list of movies.

The first line of code sets the loop of duplication by stating "while *n* is less than total, do this (rest of code)."

n is a blank variable that represents the number 0 at the beginning of the script, but on the second line, n = (n)+1;, n is added to 1. What happens with this in place after the while statement is exactly that (n = n + 1). While the loop is still in flux, the variable n is constantly changing. Every time the code is looped, it adds 1 to the variable of n. If the while statement has looped 3 times, n's actual sum will be? You guessed it! 3.

bn is a variable containing the text dup + n, which when going through the loop statement has an outcome of dup1, dup2, dup3, and so on.

dup is the instance name of the button movie clip that contains the text field and the invisible button.

The next line of code is the actual duplication.

```
duplicateMovieClip ("dup", bn, n);
```

This preceding code sets the new name of each duplicated movie clip to the variable bn that was established previously in the script.

The next line in the script is where the positioning of each clip happens after being duplicated. In this case, it gets the y position of the last duplicated movie clip, adds it to the variable n multiplied by the height of the last movie clip duplicated.

The multiplication is present because you want to make sure the next movie clip is placed at the end of the list; by multiplying n by the height, you get the result of all the duplicated movie clips' y position. Easy as pie.

```
setProperty (bn, _y, (getProperty(bn, _y))+n*(getProperty(bn,
  _height))));
```

The very last line of script sets the variable dupH on the main timeline that contains the exact height of every movie clip that was duplicated. This variable is used only for the scrolling script in the control movie clip to know when scrolling has reached the bottom.

Although it seems rather boring, this last bit of code is what makes the scroller worthwhile. It always knows when to stop the scrolling before everything just zooms off the screen. Just think, if you have ever made a scroller before, you have probably, at one point or another, put in hard code to stop movement of your movie clip. This is totally worth your time.

```
root:dupH = _parent.roller.dup._height*total;
```

Well, that's how it works. The names, links, and total for the duplication method can be found in the text files on the CD. All that is needed is to replace any content with your own and off you go.

Again, if you have questions regarding ActionScript, the Flash Help file is the first place you should look. Don't worry, this is the most scripting this book goes over. If you're hungry for more, however, the best pacifier is to scrounge through others' code to see how they did it.

with This or That

Remember Flash 4 and the TellTarget ActionScript element? Well, it caused quite a stir with designers and developers alike when it was released with Macromedia's preceding version. There wasn't a Flash message board on the Web that didn't have at least five new entries a day asking for help with it.

Just to catch you up, if you haven't had the pleasure of working with Flash 5, the ActionScript element that is replacing the ever-popular TellTarget is called with. It seems that most in the Flash community have grasped the logic behind it; for sanity's sake, however, this section reviews it because it was such a trouble spot before and because we use it briefly with the navigation's scroll arrows and scroll control movie clip.

with is the ActionScript element to use if you have a movie clip that needs to control another movie clip. Basically it is used as a pointer to tell a certain movie clip to play, skip to a frame, or even play another movie clip inside itself. For example, if the user does this with thisMovieClip, do this.

To get a better understanding of with, take a look at the actions for the down scroll arrow for the navigation in the main movie.

```
on (press) {
     with(control) {
          gotoAndPlay (2);
     }
}
on (release) {
     with(control) {
          gotoAndStop (1);
     }
}
```

In its simplest form, the preceding script tells the control movie clip to go to and play frame 2 if the button is pressed; and if the button is released, it tells control to go to frame 1 and stop. It is really quite simple once you gasp its logic.

Also, when dealing with the with statement, think of your hierarchy as well. Imagine that the control movie clip is inside of another movie clip named totalControl and has an instance with the same name. Targeting for control would change based on where it is located.

The following code shows the changes:

```
on (press) {
     with(totalControl.control) {
          gotoAndPlay (2);
     }
}
```

Basically you would need to change the path to the movie clip you want to control. Even easier, huh?

Both of the arrows for the navigation in the main movie have the with statement, as do the keyframes within the control movie clip. Looking through the supplied source code will definitely help you understand this method and will hopefully lead you down a path of more complex possibilities of interaction between movie clips.

loadMovie

The scenes are ready, the layers are set, and the library is waiting. Tackle the functionality of how the employee templates will display by using a small feature within Flash ActionScripting that has proven itself again and again to be the savior of many a large site. (We even gave it its own section!) Again, if you are not too familiar with setting actions or keyframes, or with general Flash usage, you should review the lessons that came with Flash 5 before continuing with the rest of this chapter.

Now then, the reason for the loadMovie action: On a fast connection, users rarely notice its use; but on a slow connection, its transitions save the download day. Sure you could build a site completely in one Flash file—one file, no clutter—but this method would fail horribly because having to wait for a 2MB file to load over a dial-up Internet connection is just silly. If you can possibly chop that same movie into smaller pieces that load only when the user requests the information, the experience of the site will only be enhanced. To further explain: When the URL of the main document is called, only the main movie loads. Based on what the user chooses from the main movie's navigation, another movie will load into the main movie. This allows for an almost seamless way to fuse movies together and for transitions to be utilized to their fullest—as opposed to going to a new URL and waiting for anything... anything at all to show up.

What this basically means is that a scene that could normally be set up to have set content will behave just as a shell for multiple sets of content. For example, once the user action of selecting an employee is determined, the movie goes to the specified scene and calls the appropriate movie to be loaded. Simple enough, huh?

note

Size Counts. When designing or laying out movies that will be used by the loadMovie action, the "sister" movie that will by loaded/unloaded (in this case, the employee templates), should be of equal size and frame rate.

Before delving into the example of the code used in conjunction with the duplication menu, consider the basics of loadMovie. An average loadMovie script should look like this:

```
loadMovieNum ("emp17.swf", 20);
```

One thing to notice is that the preceding code example contains an actual filename. For the employee templates, an expression with a variable will be used based on the instance name of the duplicated movie in which the button resides. Variables for the Generator templates are discussed later in the chapter.

An average unloadMovie script should look like this:

```
unloadMovieNum (20);
```

This example shows that that the movie previously loaded onto level 20 is the very movie that is being removed. Note that the level number is the same level number specified in the loadMovie action. This is because you want to remove the exact movie from the exact level before returning to the main navigation.

For the employee templates, the approach is similar yet a bit more complex (by the way of retrieving a variable from a text file). Take a look at the invisible button inside the main movie's navigation.

```
on (press) {
    loadMovieNum (eval("_parent.Link"+_name), 20);
}
```

In the preceding example, notice that we are still loading a movie the same way as the previous example; but we don't use an actual name for the movie to be loaded. This is because the movie titles for the employees are loaded through a text file to match up with their respective duplication name (see "duplicateMovieClip" earlier in this chapter), which is also determined by the duplication method.

To make it simple, when someone presses the button, it loads a variable that contains the correct movie clip for the person listed. To make this work, we use script element eval to retrieve the name of the variable listed in the parentheses directly after its use (("_parent.Link"+_name)). The parent.Link section basically calls where the link was loaded into the movie from a text file and the +name section appends the current movie clip instance name to the end of the string. (See Figure 4.11.)

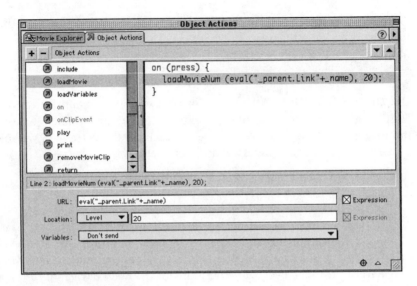

FIGURE 4.11   *Adding a loadMovie action.*

To make all this easier to comprehend, let's deconstruct how this variable is loaded into the movie. Basically, this loads the movie variable equivalent to parent.Linkdup3. If your movie in the text variable of Linkdup3 was WONDERFUL.SWF, then that's exactly what the movie would load.

This works because of the duplication method mentioned previously. In the duplication method, you set each newly duplicated movie clip with a name of dup. Each time the duplication script loops, it changes the variable of *n*, which is appended to the end of each of the duplicated movie clips as well, creating a series of movie clips with names such as dup0, dup1, dup2, and so on. This is how the text file should be set up to represent each of the employees within the navigation. In the link text file, the variables for each of the employee movies is the same as its duplicated instance, but with Link appended to the beginning. They look like Linkdup0, Linkdup1, Linkdup2, and so on.

It's all coming together now, right? Well, if it seems a bit out of the way, everything for the duplication script including the buttons is in the source file for the taking. Use it, mutilate it, and alter it until you have a wonderful headache and cannot see straight.

Now, all that is left to do is to plug any other specific actions you may have to contribute and you will be ready to go to work. You are a couple of steps closer to the finished template. To help you even further along with the actions, you can find all actions that pertain to the employee site navigation in Appendix A. The appendix lists every action for control, duplication, load variables, and the button. These are provided so that you can reference them without opening a Flash file. You should still work within the file to see how they were placed according to an actual timeline that shows the hierarchy of the instances they reference.

As simple as the `loadMovie/unloadMovie` commands are, they play a huge role by helping you manage and display the employee movies. Again, use the code from the source if ActionScripting isn't your cup of java.

Image and Sound Optimization

Because you will be using images in the employee templates, why not go over optimization before getting into an overstuffed file? After all, images/bitmaps are of special concern when dealing with Generator and Flash (due to internal compression).

Over time, most designers and developers of Internet media and content have learned to optimize images that will be displayed through telephone lines without causing complete gridlock. Designing for Flash is no different. In fact, going about the daily routine of optimizing images as one normally would is still the best bet.

In an informal test of Generator's optimization of JPGs, the results were quite astounding. Consider this test. First, take a single image and save it with three different JPEG qualities in Photoshop, Image Ready, and Fireworks (three of each, a total of nine). Then test those images with three different compression settings within Generator. The conclusion is that Generator's compression setting should match the original files' compression as close as possible. In some cases, using the 100% default compression with Generator actually doubles the original file size.

The Photoshop Example

The Photoshop images with various JPEG compression sizes before output with Generator:

- Image 1 with 100% (12 JPEG quality) compression file size: 401K
- Image 2 with 70% (7 JPEG quality) compression file size: 78K
- Image 3 with 40% (4 JPEG quality) compression file size: 53K

Generator Output

At 100% JPEG quality:

- Flash movie 1 generated with 100% JPEG quality (Flash internal settings) using Image1: 283K

- Flash movie 2 generated with 100% JPEG quality (Flash internal settings) using Image 2: 210K

- Flash movie 3 generated with 100% JPEG quality (Flash internal settings) using Image 3: 167K

At 70% JPEG quality:

- Flash movie 4 generated with 70% JPEG quality (Flash internal settings) using Image1: 51K

- Flash movie 5 generated with 70% JPEG quality (Flash internal settings) using Image 2: 52K

- Flash movie 6 generated with 70% JPEG quality (Flash internal settings) using Image 2: 48K

At 50% JPEG quality:

- Flash movie 7 generated with 50% JPEG quality (Flash internal settings) using Image1: 48K

- Flash movie 8 generated with 50% JPEG quality (Flash internal settings) using Image 2: 39K

- Flash movie 9 generated with 50% JPEG quality (Flash internal settings) using Image 3: 39K

So, to achieve the best results, optimize images normally and match the Generator compression as best as possible. If the original image is saved with a 7 JPEG quality, Generator's JPEG compression should be 70% to 75%. Images are not equal to each other, so optimizing all your images the same can sometimes throw the file size for a loop. Again, just remember to optimize before you generate.

Images imported straight into Flash have a slightly different spin than those brought into Generator. When images are imported into Flash, that's it, the compression they came in with is the compression they will use—unless the file seems unruly with its size. When this occurs, the first thing to do is to check the original image in whatever image-editing software was used to create it (Photoshop works well) and reduce the image quality setting, remove colors, whatever you have to do to get it down to the size you need. If this just will not do, because of design restraints or if it will alter the image beyond what would normally be perceived (in your eyes) as a good image, you have one last hope: the Image Properties panel.

To open the property panel of the image, you must first open the library. Select Window/Library. Find the image that needs to be adjusted (in this case, a JPG). Select it and click the properties icon (the blue dot with the lowercase *i* at the bottom of the library window. The Properties panel displays.

The main thing to be concerned with on this panel is the Use Document Default Quality check box. This is where the optimization occurs or doesn't occur. Uncheck it and a quality setting box will appear just beneath it. You can adjust the quality of the image compression here; but how much is totally based on the image in question. Do not select Lossless from the drop-down list if the image is a JPG; the size can jump from 52K to 238K in a heartbeat and make a grown person cry! (See Figure 4.12.)

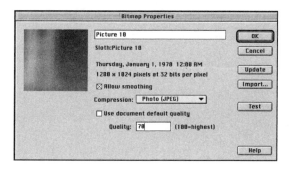

FIGURE 4.12   *The Bitmap Properties panel.*

The discussion now turns to using sound with Flash.

Sound is an integral part of an interactive experience and shouldn't be taken for granted. Far too many designers and developers throw any sound into the movie and call it a day, making the file size creep well beyond what would even be considered a large file in the process. This is due to inexperience with working with Flash as a tool, the lack of preparation, and dealing with sound in general. *Wisdom is gained by doing.*

When dealing with imported sounds, the first thing that should have taken place is optimization outside of Flash with a sound editor such as Sound Edit 16, Pro Audio, Sound Forge, Sound Forge XP, and so on. Now when finalizing the sounds, take into account what the sound will be used for. Will it be a simple notification sound used for a button or other user

note

Format Choices. For images of photo quality, use JPG. For images with flat, nongradient color, use GIF. And for images containing an alpha setting or transparency, use PNG. With these guidelines, the file sizes of each should be optimal.

prompted response? Will it be used for streaming background music? Will the user need to wait for the sound file to load before the movie plays? Each of these questions should be answered before actually importing sound into Flash and should be optimized accordingly before production begins.

After the sound files have been imported into Flash, further optimization can and should occur (depending on sound quality of the original).

Just as you would change the properties of an image, select the sound file in the library. Click the blue properties icon. Notice that there is a compression drop-down list toward the bottom of the panel. (See Figure 4.13.)

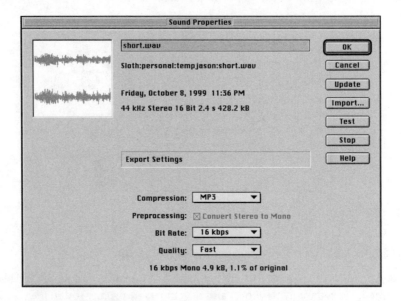

FIGURE 4.13   *The Sound Properties panel.*

With the MP3 export option, a file that has an original size of 8K can be compressed to 0.8K. This ratio is incredible, and you should use this compression with all of your movies from now on.

For the most part, choosing MP3 is the way to go for nearly all sounds. Depending on the sound quality of the original, however, you may choose another setting. All the settings are discussed more thoroughly within the Flash documentation.

Another trick that will help speed the production process and allow your site to load much faster is the use of loadMovie (discussed earlier in the chapter). Setting up a template for use only with sound is becoming an industry standard itself. It will allow for a sound file to load on its own terms—barely affecting the main movie's load time—and gives you more control over multiple sound files piled in one file.

Suppose, for example, that the main movie is loading. When it reaches a certain keyframe containing the loadMovie action, the sound template is called. It's as simple as it sounds. This is a great way for the main movie to get a head start without waiting for a huge keyframe that contains a 300K embedded sound file before the main movie can continue playing its animation sequence.

Library Organization

Before you go any further, get everything organized! One of the most overlooked and misused practices with designing/developing in Flash is the habit of keeping a clean house. The library is a key element for a Flash designer/developer (see Figure 4.14). While featuring the ease of drag and drop, a preview pane, and accessibility to all of your symbols, it can slow production time down to a crawl if you don't keep it organized. Suppose, for instance, that you are building a Flash file that will be shared with the other designers and developers working on the same project. You know that you will not make all possible changes in the future, but, at the same time, you don't want to be left in the dark if you need to work on the very same file you created months ago. Workflow will only go as smoothly as you set up the library. Keeping that in mind, how you organize your library is completely up to you as a designer/developer. However, listed here are a few points to help you evaluate how it should be set up:

- Will other designers/developers be working within the file?
- Are there key elements such as navigation, scenes, or movie clips that contain a large number of symbols that pertain only to those particular items?
- Does your workflow process already establish a naming convention?
- Months from now, will you personally have no problems reopening the file to make changes?

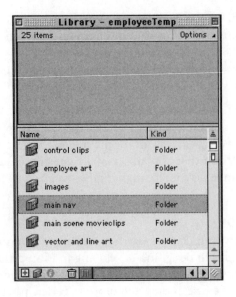

FIGURE 4.14   *The library.*

All four of the items listed closely relate to each other and all relate to folders within the library. The second point is of greater importance. Key elements such as navigation, scenes, and movie clips that contain symbols only associated within those items should have their own folder.

Macromedia has set an example by setting up their folders for items named movie clips, buttons, symbols, and sounds.

Personalized Names. Personally, I have found that using generic folder names can cause great confusion when attempting to edit the file they're set in. Using more personal names associated with the elements eases navigation inside the file.

Working with Generator Objects

By now the foundation has been laid, you have brushed up on your scripting, and the template is almost ready for its deconstruction. Don't worry if every element isn't in its final position. It will more than likely need to be tweaked a bit more before it is over; besides, it's time to meet the Generator objects.

Representing one of the seemingly more difficult elements related to Flash are the Generator objects. For a visual designer, these lovely placeholders can be an incredible eyesore; and for the novice Flash user, the site of seeing a large group of them in use on the Stage can be disheartening. You may find that the best way to view them is to imagine them as being Greek text, similar to the way your favorite illustration or type utility displays items for faster preview. Yeah, it seems silly to even mention, but as a designer, it really helps out. Just remember that they're only placeholders. Again, they're only placeholders.

To facilitate your understanding of objects, take a look at some of them. Open the Generator Objects panel by clicking Window/Generator Objects. (See Figure 4.15.) Aren't they wonderful? As you can see, an object exists for just about anything you would want to make dynamic.

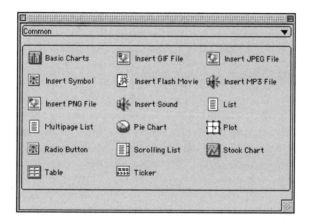

FIGURE 4.15 *Generator common objects.*

Before things go too far, it is important to explain how to utilize the objects for the employee templates. To start, consider an example of an element from the employee template. You know from the storyboards that the employee default page will have an image, so begin with that. From the Generator Objects panel, drag the JPG object to the Stage. Voilà! You can go home now (just kidding). It is simple, but there is just a bit more involved.

Now that the JPG object is on the Stage, take a look at its properties. Yep, just like everything else, it has properties. Double-click the JPG object on the Stage. The Generator panel displays. (See Figure 4.16.)

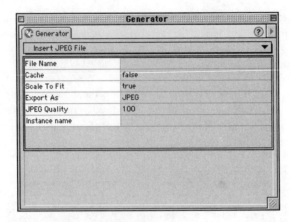

FIGURE 4.16   *The Generator object's properties panel.*

When dealing with Generator objects, the properties are of particular importance. In the JPG properties panel, you can set six attributes. Each object contains it own set of properties ranging from chart types to symbol spacing. These properties pertain only to the object selected.

The following list gives you a quick once over on setting JPG object properties:

- **File Name.** The File Name will contain the variable for the image set within the database (in this case, the employee image). It should be the same as the variable set within your ASP pages and database. This variable is discussed later in the chapter. Realize that this isn't the only way to pull an image into a template. You can actually specify MY.JPG in place of the variable and when tested it will just pop right in. This simple method will not work as smoothly with the templates, however; it just isn't dynamic enough for the mass production.

- **Cache.** The cache cannot be used with the Developer Edition, so this discussion skips on past it. (You can find more information on setting the cache either in the manual or the Flash Generator Help file.)

- **Scale To Fit.** Scale To Fit is where you will designate a true or false value. More than likely, the value will be false, unless scaling images to fit any size throughout the design is appropriate. It also is a good to note that if the size of the images is consistent throughout the site, the width and height of the Generator JPG (image) object should be reflected accordingly within the Info panel. (Such is the case with our employee images.)

- **Export As.** If you are placing a JPG, Export As is almost always going to be JPG, due to the file-compression rate. Lossless will blow up the size considerably. Refer back to the "Image and Sound Optimization" section in this chapter.

- **JPEG Quality.** Again, the JPEG Quality setting should be the same or roughly the same as the original exported JPG Quality setting. A quality setting of 7 in Photoshop will be a quality setting of 70% in Flash. Refer back to the "Image and Sound Optimization" section in this Chapter.

- **Instance name.** The Instance name, as a good rule of thumb, should be the same as the variable set within the File Name without the use of the curly braces. This creates a consistency between the two and allows for an easy call of the object with ActionScript.

> **note**
>
> **Curl Your Variables.** Again, it is important to note that all variables used with Generator must contain the curly braces so they will be recognized as a variable.

Now that there is a Generator object in the template labeled with the correct variable and other various properties, the deconstruction method rolls right up to bat. All you have to do after the object has been set up is replace the original element with the now dynamic Generator object. (See Figure 4.17.) This applies to all Generator objects, not just JPGs. See, it's as easy as pie! Generator will soon be second nature and templates will take over the world. For more information regarding specific objects and their properties, refer to the Generator Help file or the Generator manual.

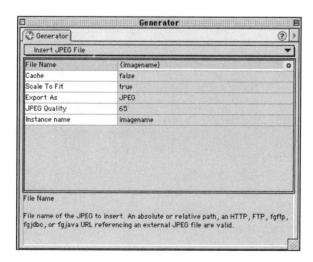

FIGURE 4.17 *Setting the variable of the JPG object within the Generator object's properties panel.*

Before you move on to throwing down the completed template, there are a few more key elements and tips to remember when working with Generator objects.

Although objects are dynamic and may contain an instance name, they are not the same as a movie clip. Effects, such as the Alpha setting, will not work directly on the objects unless they are made into their own movie clip or symbol, which can then be changed using the Effects panel. Basically, Generator objects are treated as any other design element that hasn't been made into a symbol; you cannot select anything from the Effects panel drop-down list. But this is basically because straight Generator objects have their own specific properties you can set.

Another nifty feature of Generator, which doesn't deal with its objects, is that you can use it to dynamically modify your existing instances, such as your navigation movie clip or buttons. Clicking a symbol or movie clip already present brings options into the Generator panel (if it is open) with a drop-down menu containing properties that Generator can dynamically process.

As you can see in Figure 4.18, you can dynamically set tints, custom colors, alpha, brightness, transforms, replace and replicate (which acts similar to the SmartClip except it pulls content from its own data source and actually builds a movie clip based on that data). This is great for generating personal preferences for a live Flash site.

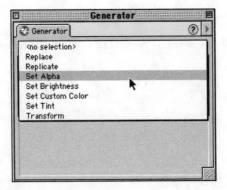

FIGURE 4.18   *The Generator properties panel also offers properties for movie clips that are not specifically Generator objects.*

For the most part, these properties that can be affected and altered by Generator can be re-created with ActionScript. Their use depends solely on the project and its purpose. Your decision of which method to use is the only boundary.

Step 4: Designing the Template

Up to now, you have been preparing everything for the template process. Now it is time to implement what has been covered by creating the working employee templates. The time for deconstruction has arrived.

The Goals of the Templates

The goals when creating templates are as follows:

- To re-create the look and feel based on the initial design
- To set up standards throughout the site with regard to common placement of dynamic as well as static content
- To save yourself from the tremendous headache of reproducing page after page of similar content and design over and over again
- To organize workflow and utilize standards regarding production and implementation

Incorporating Dynamic Content

Well, the time has come to change the beautifully designed Flash movie into a precisely laid out template. The good news is that it is already done (for the most part). By completing all necessary tweening/animation and other aspects of the design process, the template will practically build itself. The animation, of course, was left entirely up to you and your skills acquired from working with Flash. If more needs to be done, however, by all means get everything into some type of stable condition of your preference before moving on. The reason for having everything, such as the layout and animation, close to the finished product is that there will be a replacement of items throughout the Flash file. Everything that is to be dynamic should be laid out first before continuing with the chapter.

Now all that is left to do is replace key design elements as either Generator objects or dynamic text fields. Ready?

Okay, start with an evaluation of the design. Compare it to the original storyboard and check to make sure the soon-to-be dynamic elements are ready for this process:

- Are all areas of the design flushed out and functional, as far as animation and placement go?
- Is the animation timed according to the wireframes, and is it comfortable?
- Does the movie fit the client?
- Are there action layers present where applicable?

If these four questions can be answered with yes, the movie is ready. Otherwise a bit more tweaking is in order. One of the main reasons developing in Flash can bog down as it gets further along is that changes may be in order before you actually need them. Personal decisions and feelings regarding the animation and placement also affect the production time, usually just by being thought about too much.

One more thing: The animation is key here. If everything has been animated prior to actually replacing items with dynamic content, the library already contains symbols. Changing them to dynamic elements will be a snap. If the template is being built as a nonvisual template, it is still a good idea to have the animation finished first (especially because positioning is sometimes altered by the use of both Generator objects and dynamic text fields).

Glad we got that out of the way. Going back to the replacement of design elements and the storyboards: Notice again that the employee templates contain a total of six scenes. Remember creating them earlier in the chapter?

- Default
- Favorites
- Professional Biography
- Personal Biography
- Skills and Samples
- In Their Own Words

There are many ways to set this movie up. Because there won't be much in the way of animation/tweening, setting up a smart clip or movie clip that would contain a keyframe of each item would work nicely. However, take into account that neither will show until they're completely loaded.

A final thought on scenes: The default scene will have a similar structure to the main movie's main scene, possibly having a short intro animation that leads ultimately to a pause for information. The Professional Biography, Personal Biography, and the In Their Own Words sections will contain a dynamic text field. Finally, the Skills and Samples and Favorites scenes will contain multiple dynamic text fields.

Now take a look at the dynamic elements for the default scene specified in Chapter 2 "Designing Beyond Look and Feel," and on the storyboards. You have five dynamic elements to work with:

- Employee Photo
- Employee Name (two parts: first and last)
- Employee Title
- Employee Birthday
- Employee Hometown

Because you are already familiar with Generator objects, go ahead and use one; you'll get to the dynamic text in just a moment. Again, referring back to the "Working with Generator Objects" section of the chapter, note that you just need to drag the object from the Objects panel onto the stage and frame where the image lives. If the image is inside of a movie clip, the best thing to do is Edit in Place (discussed earlier in this chapter) and then drag the Generator object onto the Stage. Once the JPEG object is in the movie clip or on the Stage, its properties will need to be set according to how it will behave. First, however, get it into position by using the Info panel.

note

Save Time, See Context. Edit in Place saves so much time it's unbelievable. It basically takes all the guesswork out of positioning by enabling you to see the symbol/movie clip/button in context with the rest of the site.

Utilizing the Info panel when positioning elements on the Stage is crucial, especially when working with dynamic content. By specifying exact width, height, and X and Y coordinates within the Info panel, any element being dealt with will easily fall into place under your complete control, making it a breeze to replace items with new items in the exact position and the correct sizes intended.

Go ahead and select the original image and click the Info Panel tab if it is already displayed. If it isn't, go to Window/Panel and select Info. Take note of the width, height, and X and Y coordinates of the image. These will be applied to the Generator object so that it will be in the same position and be the same size as the original. (See Figure 4.19.)

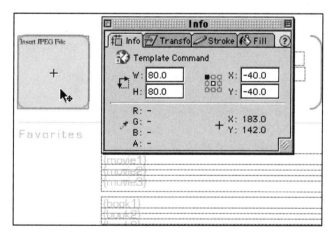

FIGURE 4.19   *The Info panel offers the option to change the dimensions of an object to a precise size.*

Now select the original image; it can now be deleted from the Stage and out of the movie clip. After clearing the Stage of the original, select the Generator object. Its Info properties should be displayed. In the Info panel, fill in the appropriate coordinates. The Generator object should now be in position of the dearly departed original. All that remains for this object is to fill out the Generator panel properties of the JPG object.

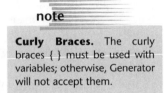

note

Curly Braces. The curly braces { } must be used with variables; otherwise, Generator will not accept them.

Do a quick refresher of a few of the properties associated with the JPG object pertaining to the employee template. Go ahead and pull up the Generator panel if it isn't already (Window/Panels/Generator or double-click the object on the screen).

For the File Name, use a variable. As previously mentioned, this variable is the link to the database and should be named accordingly with that in mind. So, use an abbreviated form of what the item actually is. Call it {imagename}. Using the curly braces, the File Name field should appear as follows:

```
{imagename}
```

Because all the images for the employee site have the same dimensions, the Scale To Fit drop down will be false. If they were different sizes, the same would hold true. (In fact, I haven't found that much use for the True selection. Maybe I'm just fond of my images remaining intact and unaltered.)

Do not change Export As. It should remain as JPEG.

JPEG Quality, as mentioned in the "Image and Sound Optimization" section in this chapter, will be 65% because for this site, the employee photos were saved as 65% JPEGs using Fireworks 3.

Incorporating Dynamic Text

One dynamic element down, how hard was that? With Generator objects behind you, you can tackle the most used dynamic element in the production of Generator templates, the dynamic text field.

Go on down the list and start with the whole employee name (see Figures 4.20 and 4.21).

Figure 4.20 *The employee name layout prior to changing to a Generator variable.*

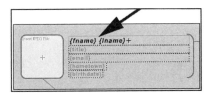

FIGURE 4.21 *Replacing the employee name from the layout with a Generator variable.*

Now, while the text is selected, open the Text Options panel if it is not open already.

To open or switch to the Text Options Panel (Mac and PC), go to the Application menu, and select Window/Panels/Text Options.

From the first drop-down list, select Dynamic Text. Static text will not return any variable. From the second drop-down list, select Single Line. (See Figure 4.22.) One thing to take note of is that the single-line dynamic text in Flash will not wrap. In fact, any extra characters that fall outside of the specified bounding box will not appear at all and will make your work seem broken and, not to mention, in the case of the employee name, make someone with an extremely long name a bit irate.

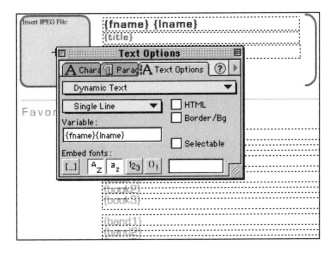

FIGURE 4.22 *Setting the employee name variables for Generator in the Text panel.*

While the Text Options panel is still open (good practice to keep it open constantly), make sure that the Selectable check box is not checked. It would not be bad if it were selected, but a bit of designer sophistication never hurt anyone.

On the subject of type, go ahead and select which characters to embed. You know that the names won't have numbers; special characters may be of need, however, and they can be entered manually in the bottom-left box. Selecting the outlines for Uppercase and Lowercase are a given unless the design calls for all of one or the other, and numbers and punctuation should not be checked. The less you have checked, the smaller file size the template will have because it won't have to carry the entire font information. This is especially true for larger font families such as Helvetica and Arial that contain full character sets.

With the new variable name (plus the curly braces) in place of the original, you're done. Each of the single-lined text fields throughout the employee site will be produced the same way.

Before you call it a day and pack everything up, consider multiple-line text fields. Don't worry, there isn't much.

Go to one of the biography scenes. If you haven't already done so, replace the design copy with a new text field by clicking and dragging with the text tool until the desired size is met.

Just as before, you need to set the variable for the text field. Replace the copy with the variable exactly as in the single-line text field example.

While the Text Options panel is still open, jump on in. With the text field selected, again select Dynamic Text from the drop-down list in the Text Options panel. Next, the drop-down list just below should be changed to Multiple. You should then uncheck the Selectable box just as before. (See Figure 4.23.) Again, violà! It is finished.

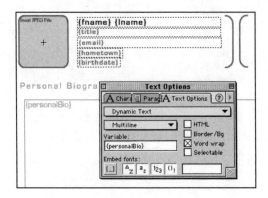

FIGURE 4.23   *Setting the personal biography variable on the Stage and in the dynamic text field in the Text panel.*

By following the examples set out within this chapter, you should be able to finish the employee templates without a hitch. But get ready, data-entry tool considerations are next (Chapter 5, "The Data-Entry Tool"). The next chapter covers the variables mentioned here.

After going through any chapter in this book, your templates may need some tweaking here and there. The key is to not get discouraged if something seems out of whack. Just remember that you are in control; you make things happen. This is the nature of our profession.

Library Organization Revisited

After all the required elements have been reproduced in the templates, it may be time again to revisit the library. Putting everything in its proper folder and creating new folders for any additional elements created since initially starting your library are of extreme importance. It may seem tedious, even boring. When the time comes for editing your template, however, wouldn't it be nice to be able to find everything quickly?

Make an extra folder for items not in use, making sure that they are not mixed in with the actual elements being used. This is especially important for symbols of which you may have duplicates. (See Figure 4.24.)

Figure 4.24   *The organized library.*

Cleaning House: Ridding the Template of All the Extras

When the template is complete and you feel that it is ready to go out on its own to make a living, you might want to tidy it up and remove excess baggage. Remember all the small things you accumulated as a child? Well, your template will remember everything it has accumulated as well. Personally, I find no reason to carry everything I own everywhere I go, so I usually pack things up and hide them in storage until I need them later or just want to take a walk down memory lane.

Ridding your template of extraneous items no longer in use will help keep your file clean and healthy. Extra images, duplicate movie clips, extra lines, guide layers, empty layers, and shapes that you know are not being used by the template should be deleted from the library and Stage, but before that you should save the file with a different name (for instance, TEMPLATE_OLD1.FLA or TEMPLATE_OLD2.FLA). By doing this you increase the chances of success when attempting to modify the most current file and create a working archive of work related to the specific project that you can reference anytime. Most designers/developers practice this. Just thought it was worth mentioning.

Chapter Summary

In this chapter, you explored the following topics:

- Common practices and conventions used in template design
- The importance for optimizing content to improve performance
- Standard conventions for organizing Flash movies and templates
- An introduction to Generator objects
- The use of dynamic content in the template design
- Building the employee site templates

Building the template is an extension of creating a standard Flash movie. This chapter discussed the principles and practices of organizing, optimizing, and working with dynamic content in creating a Flash template for the employee site. In building the employee page templates, you were introduced to the Generator objects and shown how to incorporate them into the design. At this point, the database and template are complete. The final piece to the puzzle is the actual content. In the next chapter, you build a tool to capture and organize this content for use in the template.

CHAPTER 5

The Data-Entry Tool

The preceding chapter discussed the development of the template used in Generator and offline-mode development. This chapter covers the final piece of the three main elements in the workflow process: the data-entry application. While you wrap up work on the template covered in the preceding chapter, you can simultaneously move ahead to the tasks described in this chapter, constructing the data-entry application. The Web-based application utilizes basic form elements such as text fields, radio buttons, scrolling lists, and selection boxes. It also connects to the database via Active Server Pages (ASPs). In this chapter, you learn ways to improve and speed up data entry for clean organized results. Finally, you will see how the data-entry Web application interacts with templates enabling you to preview and finalize template processing development. Let's get to work!

This chapter introduces you to the data-entry tool, the fifth in a six-step workflow process using offline Generator. In particular, this chapter covers the following topics:

- Defining the data-entry tools
- Understanding clean and clear data entry
- Identifying variable elements of the design (the use of server-side scripting)
- Building the data-entry tool
- Previewing content
- Planning for final production

Organizing Data

Building a data-entry tool seems at first like unnecessary extra work. After all, you are about to build an entire Flash site. What's the purpose of building an additional data-entry site? The reality is, it is an essential, if not key part of the process because content is the meat of the project. It is what differentiates the final Flash movies from each other and gives them definition. After all, without content, the templates are just incomplete empty shells. Remember too, that the streamlined site development process strongly relies on synchronized efforts in design, development, and content. A good data-entry tool not only allows these multiple tasks to occur simultaneously, but also to be perfected.

A data-entry application alone will not guarantee a streamlined process or organization of your data. It is very important to listen to the editors and designers to build an interface that works for everyone on the development team. Something to consider before you build the data-entry application is providing a set of guidelines around the data itself. Without some sort of data parameters to work from, for example, it is very likely that the content will arrive with various character lengths and styles, as illustrated in Table 5.1.

Table 5.1   Example Content Entered by Employees Under "Job Title"

Employee1 Title	Creative Director
Employee2 Title	artist
Employee3 Title	3d-animation artist, specializing in character animation and caricature illustrations
Employee4 Title	Graphic Art, Illustration, Flash, Director, Video/Sound Editing, Typography, and interface design

Using the same content supplied in the preceding table, you could give everyone a content style guide (data types, character limits, line limits, and so on) and have them resubmit their data, or you could take an average sample of the content submitted. Either way, the process is flawed. If content is resubmitted, you waste time reworking a process. And if you take an average sample of what was submitted, the content may be misinterpreted or abrupt. In both cases, you end up having to adjust some of the content to fit the new design or rework some of the design to accommodate the content. In the worst case, the reworking of processes may occur over and over again.

The key to good data entry is knowledge of the variable data fields in the database and the manner in which that data is entered into the data-entry tool. Much of this comes from your understanding of the data, as discussed in Chapter 3, "Developing the Database." For example, knowing that the Employee First Name field is limited to 50 characters on a single line, and that the Employee Personal Biography field will contain a paragraph of text limited to 5 lines, means that the data-entry fields should visually indicate this. Taking it even further, if you know that the Employee Title field can be limited to six choices, you can easily indicate this as well. It does not take long to see that this approach speeds up overall site production by structuring content entry that appropriately fits approved designs.

Later, you will use this same tool to preview content within the design instantly, thereby improving content entry further. The simple matter of previewing enables content editors to rework the data over and over, and instantly preview it in the final design. There are no wasted steps in design and/or development with each change in content.

Clean Data Entry

The goal of data entry is simplicity. Good authoring interfaces allow for clean and easy data input. They present the data (content) and its placement in the final design in a clear and straightforward manner. Good data entry comes from communication with the content editors (data-entry guys and gals) and the designer(s). If content editors need to ask where certain data gets entered, or, conversely, what some data-entry field is for, you are not achieving your goals. Likewise, if a designer creates an element or effect in Flash that cannot be executed because of the way data is input, the data-entry tool you have built has again failed its intended goal. To illustrate this better, consider the following examples in the following sections.

Example 1: Clear Placement and Realistic Data Entry

The template will contain room for an employee personal message. The database defines this field type as a Memo. A Memo field can contain up to 32,000 characters; in the design, however, you have determined that the field can fit only 300 characters in 6 lines.

In this example, you should display an Entry field that represents as much as possible the final data in the design. For this reason, a simple text form field element will not do. Although you could allow for a maximum of 300 characters with this form type, it does not appropriately reflect the final design. On top of that, as illustrated here, the text will scroll past the viewable area.

```
Single line text input:
<br>
<input type="text" name="personal_message" value="<%= RS
("personal_message") %>" size="25" maxlength="300">
```

The preceding code displays in the data-entry tool as in Figure 5.1.

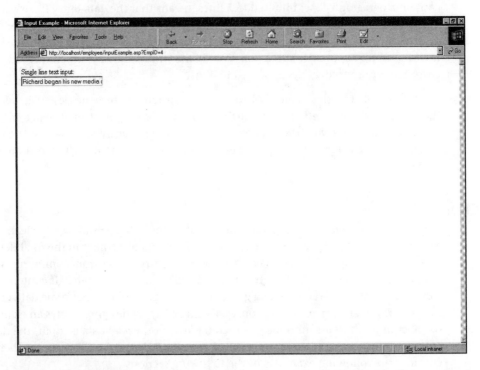

FIGURE 5.1   *This data-entry field does not display the appropriate amount of space allowed for the content being entered.*

Here is a better way to implement the Data-Entry field.

```
Multi-line text input:
<br>
<textarea name="personal_message" cols="60" rows="6" wrap="virtual"><%=
RS("personal_message") %></textarea>
```

This time, the preceding code displays in the data-entry tool more appropriately, as in Figure 5.2.

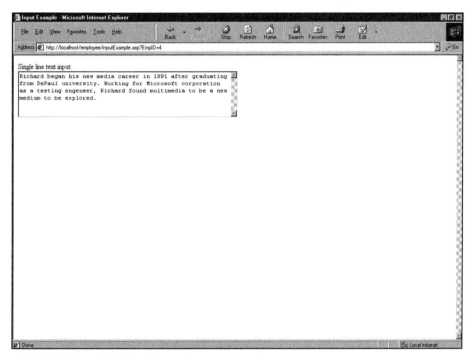

FIGURE 5.2   *This data-entry field shows more realistic spacing for the content being entered.*

Now consider the next example.

Example 2: Flash Effect

As you enter an employee page, the employee name moves across the screen.

Employee first name: 18pt Arial, alpha 30%, moving left to right, 10 pixels below employee last name.

Employee last name: 36pt Arial, alpha 30%, moving right to left, 10 pixels above employee first name.

If the data-entry tool contains only one input field for employee name, the effect illustrated here cannot occur, or at least not easily. To make this work, you must parse through the name string programmatically and search for the employee first name. You might be able to do this by looping through the name string until you encounter a space. After finding the employee first name substring match, you would have set it to a variable created to hold the employee first name. Then parse through the remaining length of the string (making sure not to include the space) and set it to a second variable for the employee last name. Keep in mind, however, that names (especially last names such as Van Slyke, for instance, which include an embedded space) cause major headaches. Of course, as noted in Chapter 3, issues such as how many and what type of data fields should already be determined by the time you have built the data-entry tool.

Identifying Elements of the Data-Entry Tool

With simplicity and easy data entry in mind, take a look at the final list of sections determined by the brainstorming sessions once again. This way you can identify all the data elements that need to be captured by the data-entry tool for those particular pages. After those elements are found, this chapter takes an in-depth look at the code needed to create them.

- Main Navigation
- Employee Default Page
- Professional Biography
- Personal Biography
- Skills and Samples
- In Their Own Words

The Main Navigation Page

The Main Navigation page will be a static page in the sense that it will not be generated using variable content from a database. Because there is only one version of this page, there really is no need for it to be created dynamically. However, a dynamic page in the future might prove useful. Consider the case for a variable navigational element that could easily adapt to employee name changes, new employees, and of course, that rare occasion when an employee leaves. We will leave that discussion for another day. For now, let's concentrate on the employee template and the input elements included there.

The Employee Default Page

As the storyboard in Chapter 2, "Designing Beyond Look and Feel," described, the Employee Default page serves as a menu to the other employee sections: Professional Biography, Personal Biography, Skill and Samples, and In Their Own Words. In addition, the storyboard calls for this page to contain an employee photo, employee information, and a list of favorites as well. Figure 5.3 illustrates what this page will look like.

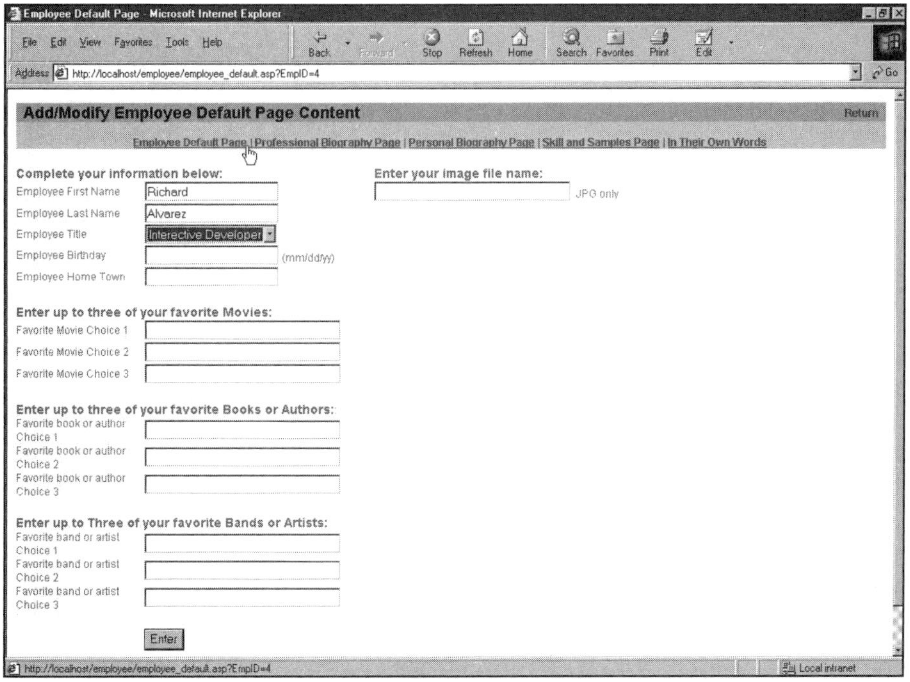

FIGURE 5.3   *The Employee Default Page contains input fields for all the required content on this page as well as links to the other content-entry pages.*

The employee photo is an easy input element to identify, but images take on a special case and a bit more coding. You will see a bit more on those specifics later in this chapter.

The following employee information also needs to be displayed in this section and subsequently will call for input fields in the data-entry tool for the following pieces of data:

- Employee name
- Employee title
- Employee birthday
- Employee hometown

The List of Favorites section requires three unique input elements for each favorite category. The List of Favorites data elements include the following:

- Favorite movies 1
- Favorite movies 2
- Favorite movies 3
- Favorite books/authors 1
- Favorite books/authors 2
- Favorite books/authors 3
- Favorite bands/musical artists 1
- Favorite bands/musical artists 2
- Favorite bands/musical artists 3

The Skills and Samples Page

The Skills and Samples page shown here contains elements that need to be presented and entered in distinct manners. Here again is another example of where the brainstorming sessions and wire-framing tasks completed in Chapters 1, "Planning Production Before Production," and 2 save the day. You defined the Skills section to be a list of predefined company skills. This means that the input options also can be defined, making data entry quicker, easier, and cleaner. As discussed in Chapter 2, if you had allowed each employee to write his or her skills in a paragraph format, you would have encountered multiple explanations of the same skills. Although that may not appear as a problem, it does require people to spend time thinking about all the tasks and roles they play. Some people may be very thorough, whereas others might gloss over it and list just a main job function. When you give a data-entry editor exact options to enter, you speed up data entry by giving limited choice. (See Figure 5.4.)

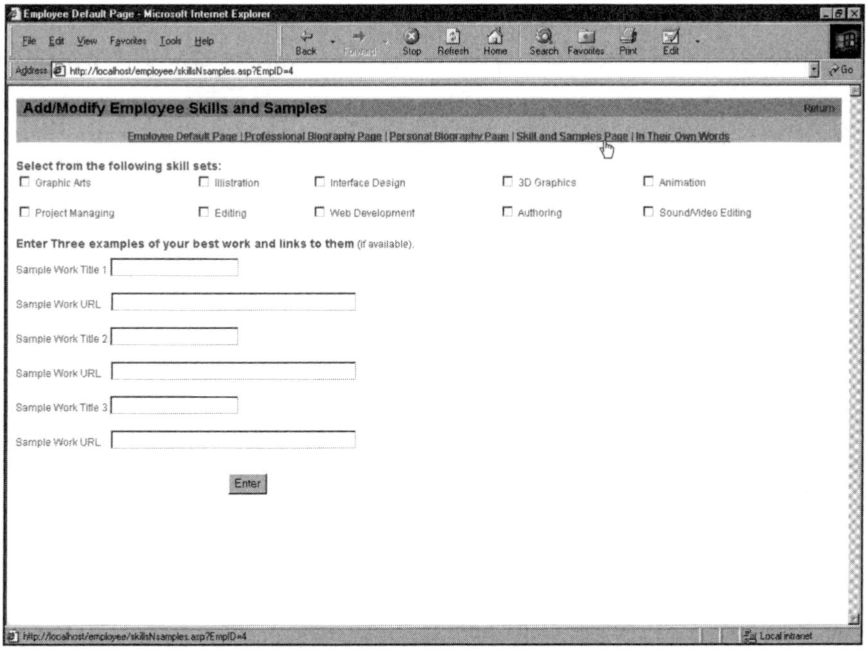

FIGURE 5.4   *The Skills and Samples page contains input fields and checkboxes for easy selection of employee skill sets.*

A list of predefined company skills follows:

Project Management

- Art director
- Administration
- Visual designer
- Motion designer
- Backend development
- Interactive development
- Media specialist
- Content editor
- Illustrator

Again, as defined in the brainstorming session from Chapter 1, employee samples will consist of three recent examples of work with links (if available). This list of samples is a unique data element because on the surface you see only the single variable element, a title identifying each sample. In actuality, each sample requires an additional hyperlink element to view it.

The Skills and Samples data elements are as follows:

- Skills from the predefined list of company skills
- Sample title 1
- Sample URL 1
- Sample title 2
- Sample URL 2
- Sample title 3
- Sample URL 3

The Professional Biography, Personal Biography, and In Their Own Words Pages

The last three pages in the employee site shown in the following figures (Professional Biography, Personal Biography, and In Their Own Words) are straightforward. Each will contain a single variable element consisting of a short paragraph or essay.

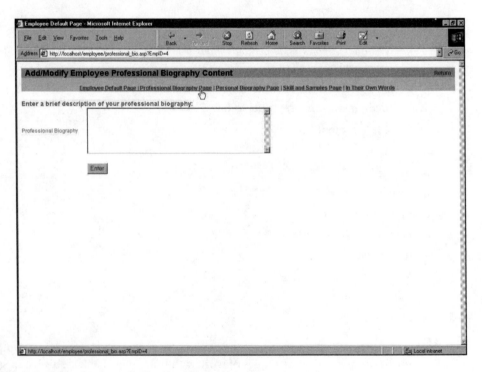

FIGURE 5.5   *The Employee Professional Biography page.*

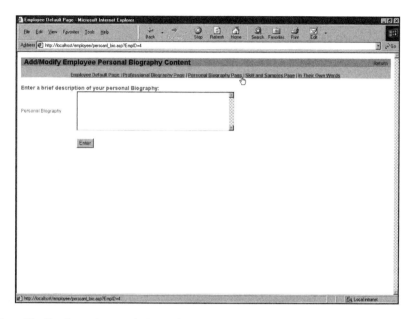

FIGURE 5.6   *The Employee Personal Biography page.*

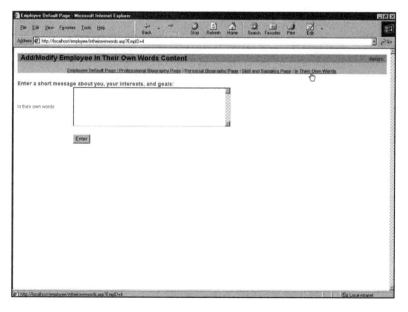

FIGURE 5.7   *The Employee In Their Own Words page.*

The Professional Biography, Personal Biography, and In Their Own Words data elements consist of the following:

- Professional Biography short essay
- Personal Biography short essay
- In Their Own Words short essay

Server-Side Scripting: ASP

The glue that binds the three components of design, development, and content together is *Active Server Pages* (ASP), a server-side scripting language. Server-side scripting can be simply described as server-generated pages that can perform server-specific tasks and in addition, call other programs to do things such as connect to data sources, perform calculations, and/or direct the browser to dynamic pages. Some examples of server-side scripting languages include Perl, ColdFusion, JSP, PHP, and Microsoft ASP. When it comes right down to it, the environment you or your client works in will help determine the choice of scripting you use. If you are in a UNIX world, for example, you may choose to use Perl, PHP, or JSP scripting. For many of us, developing for and on Windows NT servers and Microsoft Internet Information Server (IIS) is already very familiar, which makes the decision to use ASP a natural choice. Third-party vendors such as ChiliSoft and Halcyon Software's iASP enable you to develop with ASP on non-IIS Web servers. Furthermore, although ASP is usually written in VBScript, a very popular and simple scripting language, it also can be written in other languages such as JScript (a very close cousin to JavaScript) or Perl.

Here's the official Microsoft definition of ASP off of their Web site:

Active Server Pages is an open, compile-free application environment in which you can combine HTML, scripts, and reusable ActiveX server components to create dynamic and powerful Web-based business solutions. Active Server Pages enables server-side scripting for IIS with native support for both VBScript and JScript.

note

To find out more about Microsoft Active Server Pages, go to **http:// msdn.microsoft.com /workshop/server/asp /aspatoz.asp**.

Following is the list of ASP steps to display content back to the browser. (See Figure 5.8.)

1. The user visits a Web site that points to an ASP Web page.

2. The Web browser makes a request to the Web server (IIS) for an ASP file.

3. The ASP scripts on the page are processed on the server.

4. The ASP scripts are executed top down and returned as plain HTML.

5. The page is returned to the browser and displayed as plain HTML.

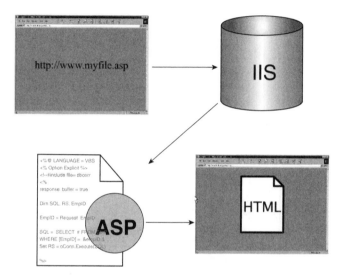

FIGURE 5.8   *The ASP steps to display content back to the browser.*

The workflow process uses ASP to glue the data between the template, the Access database, and the data source and Generator. In the data-entry tool, you use ASP to create a Web application that enables you to enter, modify, and delete data directly in the database and preview content from the templates. In addition, the offline Generator template processing will be controlled from the data-entry tool through the use of ASP scripting. You will read more about those specifics in Chapter 6, "Final Production: Putting All the Pieces Together."

The clock is ticking and every member of your staff is just itching to enter his or her own information into the Web-based data-entry application. Of course, promising a data-entry party with Chicago-style pizza helps. So enough talk, let's get into the actual construction of the data-entry tool.

The Goals of the Data-Entry Tool

The obvious reason for data entry is to capture and organize data for later use with the templates and Generator. A Web-based front end makes a great deal of sense because it is an interface that most people are already very familiar with. This means that there is no need to learn a new tool. In addition, there is no need to install new applications on *x* number of computers. Your system administrators will thank you many times over for that alone! The goal of the data-entry tool is to capture clean data in an intuitive manner and to speed up the entire site development process.

Step 5: Creating a Data-Entry Tool

Earlier, you identified the data elements for each page in the employee site during the brainstorming session (discussed in Chapter 1). In addition, in Chapter 3 you laid the groundwork for construction of the data-entry tool. Your work here begins by translating the data elements identified on these pages into appropriate HTML form objects that in turn relate to fields in the database tables.

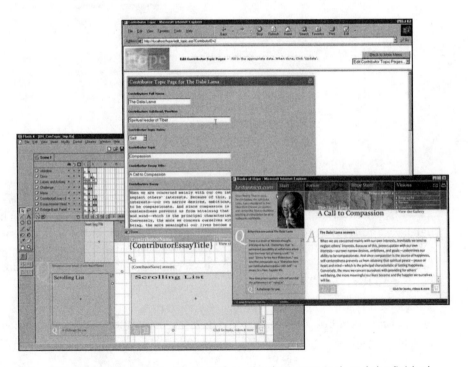

Figure 5.9   *The relationship between the template, the data-entry tool, and the finished Shockwave Flash movie.*

Essentially, three basic ASP page types make up the data-entry Web application. They are a main welcome ASP page that enables you to navigate between the different data-entry pages, an enter/modify ASP page, and an update ASP page. Each of the employee content pages (Employee Default, Professional Biography, Personal Biography, Skills and Sample, and In Their Own Words) will be of the enter/modify type.

You need to build these ASP pages:

- Welcome/Main page: DEFAULT.ASP

- Employee Default page: EMPLOYEE_DEFAULT.ASP

- Professional Biography page: PROFESSIONAL_BIO.ASP

- Personal Biography page: PERSONAL_BIO.ASP

- Skills and Samples page: SKILLSNSAMPLES.ASP

- In Their Own Words page: INTHEIROWNWORDS.ASP

- Update Content page: UPDATE.ASP

The Main Welcome Page

This page is simple and straightforward enough. It is just a jumping-off page to the other content-entry pages. (See Figure 5.10.) In the final application found on the CD-ROM, notice that this page and the rest of the data-entry pages enable you to create and delete new employee data and image uploading. For now, because you already knew exactly who was going to be entering data, the database creation team has already entered all 50 employees into the database.

The key to the Welcome/Main page is the drop-down list. It contains a list of 50 employees, which, when selected will link to the Employee Default data-entry page, the content starting point. You will use the existing records in the database to quickly populate this drop-down list with employee names by querying the database and requesting all the first and last names in the Employee table.

 note

The GET method. The code samples that follow utilize an HTML form that use the GET method, as opposed to the POST method, to pass parameters on to the server.

The HTML Form element is used to define data input. Generally, the METHOD attribute of the Form element specifies a way to access the URL specified in the ACTION attribute and is either GET or POST. When an HTML form uses the POST method to send information to the server, the parameters are sent as part of the message. An HTML form that uses the GET method, appends parameters to the URL specified in the form's Action attribute. With the GET method, a question mark (?) is used in the URL to distinguish the page address from the data parameters. For example, the following URL opens a page named MY_DATA.ASP and passes a variable named myName and a value of Richard: http://localhost/.

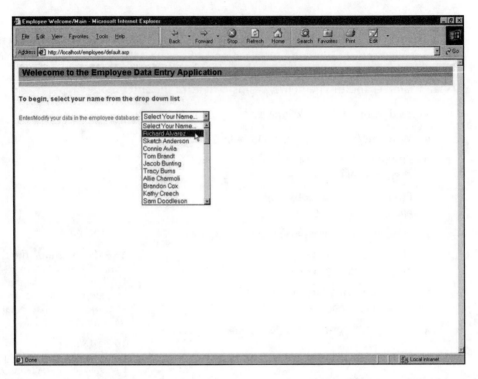

FIGURE 5.10 *The Main Welcome page serves as a navigation page for each employee content page.*

Here is the entire select-box code:

```
<select name="employees"
onChange="window.open(this.options[this.selectedIndex].value,'_self');">
  <option value="javascript:void(0)">Select Your Name...</option>
  <%
  SET Con = Server.CreateObject("ADODB.Connection")
  Con.Open "DRIVER={Microsoft Access Driver
(*.mdb)};DBQ=C:\inetpub\wwwroot\employee\employee_db.mdb"
  Dim SQL
  SQL = "SELECT EMPLOYEES.[employee_ID],EMPLOYEES.[first_name],
EMPLOYEES.[last_name] FROM EMPLOYEES ORDER by EMPLOYEES.[last_name]"
  Set RS = oConn.Execute(SQL)
  While Not RS.Eof
  %>
  <option value="employee_default.asp?EmpID=<%= RS("employee_ID")
%>"><%=
RS("first_name") %>   <%= RS("last_name") %> </option>
```

```
<%
RS.MoveNext
Wend
Set RS = Nothing
oConn.Close
%>
</select>
```

As covered in Chapter 3, each record has a unique key that identifies it. When you query the database, the resulting record set (RS) also returns this unique record key. This record key really is the key to opening the same ASP enter/modify content page with unique content from each employee. Notice that this record key is passed between content-entry pages to identify which employee content you are viewing, editing, and saving back to the database.

```
<select name="employees"
onChange="window.open(this.options[this.selectedIndex].value,'_self');">
```

The first line in the select-list box code contains the onChange() JavaScript function. It tells the browser to use the value of each selected item in the drop-down list as the page to navigate to (this.options[this.selectedIndex].value), and to load it in the same window ('_self'). Easy enough, right? Again the key, literally, comes from assigning the value of each selected item with the name of the employee default page (EMPLOYEE_DEFAULT.ASP) and the unique selected item record key. All will become clear in a bit.

```
<option value="javascript:void(0)">Select Your Name...</option>
```

In the next line of the select-list box code is the first option that appears. This item is intended for instructional purposes, and as such, it should not navigate to any page. Therefore, its value gets assigned with the empty assignment of "JavaScript: void(0). Now comes the fun part, ASP magic!

```
<%
  Dim SQL, oConn, RS
  SET oCon = Server.CreateObject("ADODB.Connection")
  oCon.Open "DRIVER={Microsoft Access Driver
(*.mdb)};DBQ=C:\inetpub\wwwroot\employee\employee_db.mdb"
  SQL = "SELECT EMPLOYEES.[employee_ID],EMPLOYEES.[first_name],
EMPLOYEES.[last_name] FROM EMPLOYEES ORDER by EMPLOYEES.[last_name]"
  Set RS = oConn.Execute(SQL)
  While Not RS.Eof
%>
```

Notice that these next few lines of code are all encased in between the ASP code brackets (<% %>). You begin by opening a connection to an Access database using a DSN-less connection. The DRIVER parameter specified in the connection Open call is included to invoke the specific Microsoft Access driver. The DBQ parameter is used to supply the path to your Microsoft Access database (MDB) file.

When an ASP Web application, such as the data-entry tool, works together with a database, it sends instructions to the OLE-DB interface, which translates and passes the instructions on to the database (or to an intervening ODBC interface, if an OLE-DB interface does not exist for your database). If the database sends a response, the OLE-DB interface translates it and passes it back to ASP Web application.

The problem is that the OLE-DB interface understands only instructions written in advanced programming languages. To get around this problem, Microsoft created ActiveX Data Objects (ADO), and made it a standard component of ASP server. This server component enables you to connect to various databases, such as Microsoft SQL Server or Microsoft Access, using Open Database Connectivity (ODBC). ODBC, in turn enables you to develop ASP scripting that can read and write data to and from a database. ADO is known as a wrapper, and its ASP role is to mask the complexity of OLE-DB.

There are actually various types of ADO connections you can invoke in your ASP scripting. The connection string and driver you use will vary depending on the type of database you use. Be sure to check the documentation for the database you are using for specific connection strings and driver specifics.

Table 5.2 shows an example of a DSN-less (ADO) connection.

Table 5.2   DSN-less (ADO) Connection

Database:	MS Access
Type:	ADO (connection string)
Example String:	DRIVER={Microsoft Access Driver (*.mdb)};DBQ=C:\inetpub\wwwroot\asp\myDatabase.mdb
String Format:	DRIVER={Microsoft Access Driver (*.mdb)};DBQ=[path to database]
DSN ADO (ODBC Data Source Name) Connection	
Database:	MS Access
Type:	ADO (ODBC Data Source Name)

DSN:	myDatabase
Username:	[username]
Password:	[password]

Next, you define a SQL variable and assign an actual SQL statement to it. In this case, you are looking to build an RS that contains all the employee IDs (the record set key!), first names, and last names in the Employee table. Oh, and one more thing, you want to have the record set returned to you in alphabetic order by last name. You do not even have to say "please." Instead you invoke the ASP oConn Com object to execute a SQL statement and assign it to an RS. Before you can say, "Easy as pie," poof, the RS is returned and you are ready to move on. And that is exactly what you will do. The next line puts the RS into action by setting up a loop that hits every record in the RS until you get to the end.

```
<option value=" employee_default.asp?EmpID=<%= RS("employee_ID") %>"><%=
RS("first_name") %>   <%= RS("last_name") %> </option>
```

At this point, you are in the middle of the loop. Here, each execution of the code is replayed for every employee (the RS). This is the meat of the code. Two very important actions are taking place, so let's take this code fragment and break it down even further.

```
<option value=" employee_default.asp?EmpID=<%= RS("employee_ID") %>">
```

This first chunk is exactly what you think it is. It is a list option in the select list box. What makes it unique, however, is the value that is being assigned to it. Remember the value of the list options is actually the page that you will link to when you select a name in the list box. The page you link to is always the same, EMPLOYEE_DEFAULT.ASP. The data that appears in that page, however, is unique. It belongs to the employee whose name is selected. You will see very soon how this and the other employee data-entry pages are built; for now, however, what you need to know is how to load an ASP page and a unique variable value. This is accomplished by passing parameters along a URL by appending variables to it. This method is used throughout the workflow process. The following syntax is used to append variables to a URL:

```
path/file.asp?var1=string1&var2&string2
```

Where var1 and var2 are the variable names and string1 and string2 are the values for the variables.

In the select box code, you will pass the variable "EmpID", with the value of the selected employee ID record key.

```
<%= RS("first_name") %>   <%= RS("last_name") %> </option>
```

The second part of the code fragment is the visual display that you see in the select box list. Notice the two sets of ASP brackets. Each contains the values of the current employees' first names and last names, respectively. As you loop through the RS, these values change to reflect the values in the current record, which brings you to the next and final code segment in the select box code.

```
<%
RS.MoveNext
Wend
Set RS = Nothing
oConn.Close
%>
```

The RS.MoveNext tells ASP to move to the next record. You process through all the records, or employees, in the record set until you hit the end. The remaining lines of code are basically housekeeping. Close the while loop, empty the RS, and finish up by closing the object connection to the database. You are such a neat fanatic. Tada, the ASP wizardry is complete. It does not matter whether you had three employees or 1,000. They all magically appear in the drop-down list and when selected, link to their appropriate content page for data entry/modification.

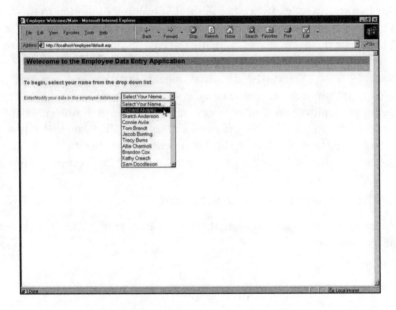

FIGURE 5.11   *The Employee Default page, ready for input and modification.*

Modify-Content Page

Notice how when you first enter an Employee Default page, the Name field is already filled in. As you fill in data and revisit these pages, the data is always remembered and displays for you. You also have included header navigation to the other employee data-entry pages for quick access. Each of these links uses the same convention of passing variables with the URLs you just learned. This simple and clean approach also gives some instructions for data entry. The Birth Date field contains the proper format to enter the date, and the Image Filename field requests a JPG file only. Further instructions should be used to ensure clean data entry without confusion. For example, you could display character limits or additional text or number formats as guides. Finally, notice the Enter button at the bottom of the page. That is the trigger that starts the update process in the data-entry tool.

All enter/modify content pages basically take on this same approach. Later in this chapter, the discussion turns to form-element specifics (such as text inputs, selections, and automatic entries). Now let's speak to the common elements of all enter/modify pages. Instead of going through the entire page, take a closer look at the essential sections of the page to understand the scripting involved. Those sections include the following:

- The database query
- The header navigation to the other data-entry pages
- Displaying content
- Form-submit action

The Database Query

This code should be recognizable from the earlier discussion on the Welcome/Main page. Does it look familiar? It should. There are really only minor differences from the preceding query you performed. Last time you built an RS that contained specific fields from all the records in the table. This time you build an RS with specific criteria containing all fields. Do not let this confuse you. Think of it this way. In the first query, you wanted to build a list of all employees. Each employee record contains his or her own attributes, name, title, birthday, and so on. That query returned only the employee ID (the key), first name, and last name of all employees. This time you want a query to return all the attributes of a single employee. Here's how it is done.

```
<%
  Dim SQL, oConn, RS
  SET oCon = Server.CreateObject("ADODB.Connection")
  oCon.Open "DRIVER={Microsoft Access Driver
(*.mdb)};DBQ=C:\inetpub\wwwroot\employee\employee_db.mdb"
  SQL ="SELECT * FROM EMPLOYEES WHERE [employee_ID] =" & Request("EmpID")
& ";"
  Set RS = oConn.Execute(SQL)
%>
```

Notice again how all the preceding code is enclosed between the ASP code brackets. The first thing you need to do is declare variables that you will be using. The SQL variable will hold the actual SQL statement. RS is a variable you will use to hold a returned RS.

Now you are ready to make the big request. The asterisk in the statement indicates that you want all the fields returned from the EMPLOYEES table. Next, ask for only certain records. In this case, the criteria you place in the request is for only those records that have an EmpID and is equal to the employee ID key. Ahhh, here is where the magic happens once more. Remember the referencing page sent a variable and value as a parameter attached in the URL. Request is an ASP statement that receives the value of the variable named "EmpID" passed in the URL. Notice the address bar and the variable and value that are passed in the URL. If the URL contains the passed parameter <?EmpID=4>, as illustrated, the completed ASP process turns the SQL statement into <SELECT * FROM EMPLOYEES WHERE [employee_ID]=4;>. The next line in the code executes a SQL statement as before, but this time the resulting RS contains all the fields in the table for only employee ID 4.

Header Navigation

The header navigation really should not be much of a challenge now that you have completed some of the other code segments. In fact, this is actually the same technique you used when you built the drop-down list box in the Welcome/Main Navigation page.

```
<div align="center">
  Employee Default Page | <a href="professional_bio.asp?EmpID=<%=
RS("employee_ID") %>">Professional Biography Page</a> | <a
href="personal_bio.asp?EmpID=<%= RS("employee_ID") %>">Personal
Biography Page</a> | <a href="skillsNsamples.asp?EmpID=<%=
RS("employee_ID") %>">Skill and Samples Page</a> | <a
href="intheirownwords.asp?EmpID=<%= RS("employee_ID") %>">In Their Own
Words</a>
</div>
```

Each menu item is linked to the appropriate data-entry enter/modify page. Again, there is really only one copy of those pages. Each time you link to it, however, you will see unique employee data displayed. Again, the trick is to pass an EmpID variable and value as a parameter in the URL.

Displaying Content

Displaying the content from the database also is very simple. Keep in mind that you have already made a SQL request and built the RS. Now all that is left to do is to reference the field names in the database from the RS. Here is the code that displays the employee first name.

```
<tr>
  <td width="150" class="navform">Employee First Name</td>
  <td width="261"> <input type="text" name="first_name"
value="<%=RS("first_name") %>"> </td>
</tr>
```

After you build a table row and column, enter the display instruction from what the following input field will contain. You have used a style sheet class for aesthetic display purposes only. It is not necessary, but it does help to keep the page cleaner. The important part comes in the next column. Remember in the database, employee first names are held in the field named "first_name". With this in mind, consider two main points about the following code.

First, the data-entry tool uses form elements—such as <input>, <select>, and <submit>—to display the data from the database. In return, these form elements are used to reference the data in the browser for possible modification back in the database. To do so properly, consistent naming of form elements and corresponding fields in the database is essential. In addition, naming form elements enables you to perform form validation on field inputs. Good to keep in mind, but out of scope for this lesson.

The second point is the use of the field name when referenced in the RS. That's it. Just use ASP to display the contents of the field in the RS. Notice how the ASP brackets open with an equal sign. This convention tells the server to return the value of ASP code to the screen for display. If the first_name field in the RS contains the value of "Richard", the following ASP code will be processed

```
<input type="text" name="first_name" value="<%=RS("first_name") %>">
```

and sent back to the browser as

```
<input type="text" name="first_name" value="Richard">
```

Form-Submit Action

Take a look at what happens when employees fill in their content and press the Enter button on the page. The Enter button is really just a submit button.

```
<input type="submit" name="Submit" value="Enter">
```

When a form is submitted, the form action is called. In this case, nothing special is going on here. The ACTION attribute in the Form tag specifies the location to which the contents of the form data fields are submitted. In this case, you can see that the form gets submitted to the update page UPDATE_EMP.ASP. In the next line of code, you pass the EmpID to the update page using a hidden input type.

```
<form name="emp_form" action="update_emp.asp" method="post">
<input type=hidden name="EmpID" value="<%= RS("employee_ID") %>">
```

Before you move on to the update page, recall that form elements are references to the data displayed in the browser. These references are used in the update page to modify the data back in the database.

Update Page

The workings of the update page happen behind the scenes. There is no visual display, only code.

```
RS.Source = "SELECT * FROM EMPLOYEES WHERE employee_ID="&
Request("EmpID") & ";"
RS.CursorType = 3
RS.LockType = 3
RS.Open
RS("first_name") = Request.form("first_name")
RS("last_name") = Request.form("last_name")
RS("title") = Request.form("title")
    .
    .
    .
RS.Update
RS.Close
Set RS = nothing
oConn.Close
Response.Redirect "default.asp"
```

The first line in the code is similar to what you have seen before—a request to build an RS with certain criteria in a SQL statement. In fact, this statement is exactly the same one you invoked in the enter/modify page. What's different are the next couple of lines that follow.

```
RS.CursorType = 3
RS.LockType = 3
RS.open
```

These next two lines of code open the database connection with certain properties. When you execute a SQL statement, the server returns a set of rows that make up the RS. The cursor type determines the way the rows in the RS are iterated through. You have four types of cursors to choose from, and each treats the data returned in the RS differently. They include the following:

- Forward only
- Static
- Dynamic
- Keyset

Another property of the record set is the lockType. The lockType determines how to lock the data in the RS when updates are being made. Again, you have four different lockTypes from which to choose. Each affects how the database handles individual updates to requests to the data and how they may overlap

- ReadOnly
- LockOptimistic
- LockPessimistic
- adLockBatchOptimistic

The first line opens an RS with a CursorType of 3. The second line opens an RS with a LockType of 3, permitting insertions or write capabilities to the database. After all those matters have been attended to, open the RS.

Now comes the actual updating. This method is simple and straightforward. There are better error-checking methods to accomplish the update process. Refer to the update pages on the CD-ROM for alternative ways to perform updates and the associated code. What you are doing is just a one-for-one substitution of the values in forms with those in the database. Notice the similar ASP `Request` call. Like the previous ASP `Request` calls that returned the value of the variable in the URL parameters, this ASP `Request` is of the type `Request.form`. As you probably guessed, this call returns the value of the form element requested.

```
RS("first_name").value = Request.form("first_name")
RS("last_name").value = Request.form("last_name")
RS("title").value = Request.form("title")
```

This code fragment is incomplete, of course. The complete code would have a line for each form-input element in the enter/modify page. Each line would substitute the RS field name value with the requested form value.

```
RS.Update
Set RS = nothing
RS.Close
oConn.Close
Response.Redirect "default.asp"
```

Finish up by invoking the `RS.update` command. This line is what actually writes the data back to the database. After that, perform more neat and tidy housecleaning, setting the RS to empty, closing it and the database connection. Finally, redirect the browser back to the Welcome/Main page.

There you have it, Welcome/Main, enter/modify, and update complete. These are the building blocks of a truly useful data-entry tool. As you begin to build and work with large-content sites, you will learn how to reuse and perfect the code to perform error checking, form validation, create data style guides, and more. These types of functionality are incorporated in the code supplied on the CD-ROM. For now, let's delve into the form elements and discuss how they are used in the tool. You already know that all the form elements and the names you give them are key to the connection between displayed data and the data source. Each of the different types of form elements is presented in HTML with subtle differences.

Content-Entry Fields

With the knowledge of the modify/edit and update pages, all that's left to do is actually enter the data. The next few sections cover how to input various kinds of data using HTML form elements such as input boxes, check boxes, and select boxes.

Text Input

When data elements were identified earlier, it was apparent that most input elements were of the text variety. In some cases, such as first name or favorite band, the text input was a single word or short phrase. In other cases, however, such as the Biographies or In Their Own Words sections, the text input was much larger.

Single Words and Short Phrases

You have already seen how short words and phrases were scripted in HTML and ASP. As stated before, input elements are named exactly the same as the fields whose values they hold. You can display the contents of the field by setting the value property to the RS field value. Just in case you have forgotten, here it is again:

```
<input type="text" name="title" value="<%=RS("title") %>">
```

Long Paragraphs

Longer text inputs require a textarea form element. The major difference between a textarea and input type=text form elements is the placement of the value. In a textarea, there is no value property. Instead, use the same RS field call as in the short-text input as the contents of the textarea tags. The code looks like this:

```
<textarea name="personal_bio" cols="50" rows="6"> <%=RS("personal_bio")
%> </textarea>
```

Image Input

The Employee Default page requires input for an employee image. Images are a tricky thing in the sense that the image filename is usually not the only piece of variable data that needs to be stored in the database. Unless all the images are exactly the same size, it is useful to store image attributes such as image width and height as well. Of course, the trickiest part to resolve is the actual physical file.

Most likely, content editors will have the image stored in various places. Some people might want to use an image from a disk/zip they have brought from home, another computer, or from a Web site. As you have already seen in Chapter 4, "Building the Template," Generator needs to have the physical location of the file passed to it for processing. Although it is possible to have images stored in various locations, in an effort to organize and speed up the workflow process, institute a rule that all images used in the employee site project should be located in the same directory on the server. This makes processing Generator templates easier to manage and quicker. With this rule set, employees will then be required to move a copy of their image(s) file into a specified image directory on the server.

The storyboard sessions in Chapter 2 also have determined that employee images all need to be sized uniformly. Your job just got simpler. Because all images need to be stored in the same place and sized the same way, all you really need to capture is the image filename. Turns out that this is just another short-text input element you have already covered.

Of course, it would be nice to have the image filename, along with its attributes (such as width, height, file type, and size) stored in the Employee database. At the same time, it also would be nice to upload the image file to the site server. Such a process would help eliminate common data-entry errors such as typos or incorrect information that directly affects the display of the images in the templates.

The techniques described here are all possible with the use of third-party ASP components. All sorts of third-party components for ASP are available for sale and as shareware. You can find everything from calendars and calculators to specialized math functions and file management. Third-party components such as Persits Software AspUpload enable an ASP application to accept, save, and manipulate files uploaded through a browser. Additional benefits include the following:

- Full ADO support to save image files into your database using ADO objects, which is simpler to code than standard ODBC

- Allow file upload from a local machine or network to the server

- The ability to strip image attributes (filename, image type, size, and dimensions) to store in your database

note

To find out more about Persits Software, Inc. AspUpload 2.1, go to **www.persits.com/**.

- MacBinary support that allows image file uploads from Macs
- Enhanced properties and methods such as `File.SaveAs`, `File.ContentType`, and `Upload.OpenFile`

Input Choices

Making data entry clean and easy is what input choices are all about. Employees do not have to struggle with how to phrase something just right. Sometimes the answers are limited to a list of choices. A good example of just this sort of limited option is the Employee Title drop down found on the Employee Default page. Because there were only 10 title choices to pick from, there is no need to make each employee type his or her title in a field. It is much cleaner and easier to have them just select it from a list. The trick is to pull the value selected and tie it back to the form element for association with the data source. Once again, the solution comes in naming the form element. Look over the code for the Employee Title drop-down list on the following Employee Default page. Notice that the fist line in the code explicitly names the `select` option. As noted previously, the name given to the form element is the same name of the field in the database.

```
<select name="title">
<option value="Project Manager" <% if RS ("title")="Project Manager"
then response.write "selected" end if %> >Project Manager</option>
<option value="Art Director" <% if RS ("title")="Art Director" then
response.write "selected" end if %> >Art Director</option>
<option value="Administration" <% if RS ("title")="Administration" then
response.write "selected" end if %> >Administration</option>
<option value="Content Editor" <% if RS ("title")="Content Editor" then
response.write "selected" end if %> >Content Editor</option>
<option value="Illustrator" <% if RS ("title")="Illustrator" then
response.write "selected" end if %> >Illustrator</option>
<option value="Visual Designer" <% if RS ("title")="Visual Designer"
then response.write "selected" end if %> >Visual Designer</option>
<option value="Motion Designer" <% if RS ("title")="Motion Designer"
then response.write "selected" end if %> >Motion Designer</option>
<option value="Backend Developer" <% if RS ("title")="Backend Developer"
then response.write "selected" end if %> >Backend Developer</option>
<option value="Interactive Developer" <% if RS("title")="Interactive
Developer" then response.write "selected" end if %> >Interactive
Developer</option>
<option value="Media Specialist" <% if RS("title")="Media Specialist"
then response.write "selected" end if %> >Media Specialist</option>
</select>
```

When employees select a title, the value of the form element "title" gets attached to it.

The `if` statement embedded within the option items is how the correct title is displayed. The current value of `"title"` determines which option item gets `"selected"` printed with it. The one that does is the one that displays in the drop-down list.

The Skills and Samples page contains a series of check boxes from which employees can quickly select. Clicking the check box on and off is not really setting data values; or is it? The trick here is that just like the check boxes, the skill options are Boolean or yes/no data types. This means they are either on or they are off. If it is on (1, or true), show the check box as checked. Otherwise, the check box appears unchecked. The simple check is accomplished using a similar ASP `if` statement, as illustrated here:

```
<input type=checkbox name="prjManger" value="true" <% if RS( "prjManger"
) then response.write "checked" end if %> >
```

Previewing Content

Now all data is collected and entered into the database. Actually, even before it is all entered, you might want to see it come alive in the designed template, right? Why? Because before you place the finished Flash movies out on your Web server, you should preview, export, and debug the template. Previewing a template enables you to see how the template looks to users in their browsers. This also is the moment when the integrity of the design is tested and made valid by all this great content that has just been entered.

This is the real beauty of the data-entry tool just built. Although it is been referred to all along as a data-"entry" tool, it can easily be used to output data as well. In the same fashion that you queried the database for user-specific criteria manipulation in the enter/modify pages, you can query for template-specific data for use in the templates. As covered in Chapter 4, you have a number of different ways to pass a data source to Generator, including a comma-delimited text file, a URL that references a comma-delimited text file, an RS from a SQL query, or a CGI script.

Here's yet another recipe for supplying data to the template and Generator processing. First, you assign a data source to the template using the Set Environment template command. This, like most of the data sources to Generator, requires the data be formatted in a particular way. (Refer to Chapter 3 for Flash 5 data source specifics.) In this case, you

> **note**
>
> **Environmentally Friendly.** The `Set Environment` command in Flash can use HTTP://, FTP://, or FILE:/// as an address to a data source. The file or source must return a text file or more specifically, data whose MIME type equals text. As mentioned before, the text also must be properly formatted. Use the `Set Environment` command from within the template, as shown in Figure 5.13.

need the data to appear in two columns. The following is a Generator text file data source showing properly formatted name value pairs:

Name	Value
Variable1,	"Value1"
Variable2,	"Value1"
Variable3,	"Value3"

Second, write some ASPs that calls the database, formats the data properly in a comma-delimited fashion, and outputs it to a text file.

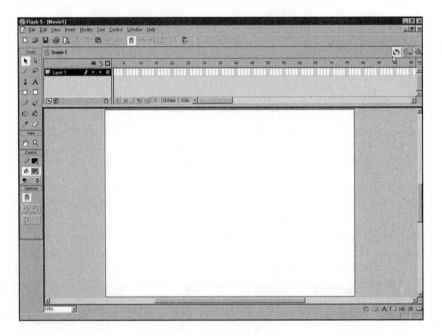

FIGURE 5.12 *Click the Generator Environment Variable button.*

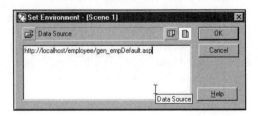

FIGURE 5.13 *Type in the URL that points to the ASP Data Source Query page.*

Okay, now take a look at the ASP code that will construct the data source and format it correctly for the template and Generator.

```
<%
Dim RS, SQL, Header, Values
SET Con = Server.CreateObject("ADODB.Connection")
  Con.Open "DRIVER={Microsoft Access Driver
(*.mdb)};DBQ=C:\inetpub\wwwroot\employee\employee_db.mdb"
SQL ="SELECT * FROM EMPLOYEES WHERE [employee_ID] =" & Request("empID") &
";"
Set RS = oConn.Execute(SQL)
Header = "Name, Value" & vbcrlf
Values = Values & "firstName, " & """" & RS("first_name") & """" & vbcrlf
Values = Values & "lastname, " & """" & RS("last_name") & """" & vbcrlf
Values = Values & "title, " & """" & RS("title") & """" & vbcrlf
Values = Values & "birthday, " & """" & RS("birthday") & """" & vbcrlf
Values = Values & "hometown, " & """" & RS("hometown") & """" & vbcrlf
Values = Values & "email, " & """" & RS("email") & """" & vbcrlf
Response.Write Header & Values
Set RS = Nothing
oConn.Close
%>
```

With the work you have done in completing the data-entry tool, the ASP code (like the one here) should be getting pretty simple. You start by defining variables that will be used later in the code. Then define a SQL statement by selecting criteria based on a specific employee by requesting an employee key from the URL parameters. Then define an RS and execute the SQL. Now you are ready to construct a properly formatted text file.

The next line builds a text string that you will use as a header. Recall that Generator requires that the data source text file be formatted with this type of header in line 1. The header will consist of the text "Name, Value". The characters vbcrlf are actually the single return-character value that tells ASP to force a new line.

Now the data source file gets some real data. The values of the employee first name, last name, title, birthday, hometown, and email are dumped into a text file to be used with the Employee Default page template. For each line of the variable Value, insert the name of the variable, the actual data value as entered by the employee, and a carriage return. The lines of code that follow get appended to the end of the Value variable. After you finish, just output the newly constructed data source text (Header and Values) using the ASP command Response.Write.

Although it may not appear to be formatted properly, if you view the source in a text editor (Windows Notepad, for instance), you will see that the file is indeed to Generator's liking and ready to use in the template (see Figure 5.14). Don't believe us? Check for yourself. The resulting output should look just like that in Figure 5.15.

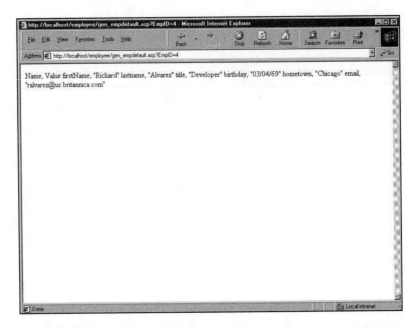

Figure 5.14   *The constructed data source text file displayed in the browser as a result of the Response.Write command.*

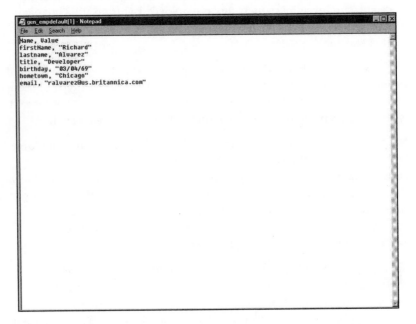

Figure 5.15   *The constructed data source text file displayed in Windows Notepad.*

Pretty cool, isn't it? There are only a few remaining pieces left to be added to the data-entry tool. You might be wondering, "How can I call a template that pulls from this data source from within the data-entry tool?" Funny you should ask. Next, you create a Preview button/link to an HTML page that calls the SWT (template file) and feeds it a unique key ID [EmpID] for previewing. The embedded SWT code takes on a very familiar coding technique:

```
<OBJECT CLASSID="clsid:D27CDB6E-AE6D-11cf-96B8-444553540000" WIDTH="760"
HEIGHT="374" CODEBASE="http://active.macromedia.com/flash5/cabs/
swflash.cab#version=5,0,0,0" id="myTemplate">
<PARAM NAME="SRC" VALUE="employeeDefault.swt?EmpID=<%= Request("EmpID")
%>">
<PARAM NAME="QUALITY" VALUE="high">

<EMBED SRC="employeeDefault.swt?EmpID=<%= Request("EmpID") %>"
WIDTH="760"
HEIGHT="374"
QUALITY="high"
PLUGINSPAGE="http://www.macromedia.com/shockwave/download/
index.cgi?P1_Prod_
Version=ShockwaveFlash">
</EMBED>

</OBJECT>
```

There are other ways to preview templates using data sources. Chapter 4 discussed some of these options. Such techniques for previewing content are essential, especially in the design and development of the template. The technique previously discussed here is most useful for all those involved in the project who are concerned with the technical or design aspects of the site. It will be most useful for content developers and site maintenance. Keep in mind that you are not testing template functionality, design visuals, or flow here. Those matters should have been taken care of by this point. If you find errors or areas that still need to be tweaked, you need to step back and address those specific areas in design and/or development of the template.

Planning for Final Generator Production

The previewing techniques shown here have laid the foundation for what you will be doing in the final production. In the same manner that you preview a template, you can actually process the template and post it onto the server for final deployment. More details on that in the next chapter.

When the preview is satisfactory, you can create the final Shockwave Flash (SWF) movie. One way to do this is to write a CGI script that invokes GENERATE.EXE and converts the template (SWT) into a Shockwave Flash (SWF). There are many ways to do this depending on your expertise with CGI. If you are like us, you are more likely to continue to work with the existing technology you are developing in ASP. At **www.serverobjects.com**, you can find free, shared, and commercial server CGI scripts that can be invoked by ASP. One that we love is AspExec. It enables you to execute DOS command-line calls from ASP; and with this, you can take advantage of offline Generator and its command-line features. This is exactly what you do in the next chapter.

Chapter Summary

In this chapter, you explored the following topics:

- **Clean and clear data.** Before you build a data-entry tool, you need to understand how the data will be displayed and used in the design. You can create cleaner data entry by giving content editors simple and intuitive input choices.
- **Active Server Pages.** Active Server Pages (ASP) is a server-side scripting language. The data-entry tool uses ASP to create a Web application that will enable you to enter, modify, and delete data directly into the database and preview content in the templates.
- **Data-entry elements.** The basic building blocks of the data-entry tool are the Welcome/Main page, the enter/modify page, and the update page. HTML form elements are used to display and reference data and data sources.
- **Data-entry tool functions.** The data-entry tool serves as a central location of content input, modification, and deletion. It can be used to preview content and speed up final production with delivery of the Shockwave Flash (SWF) movies.

In developing the employee site, hopefully you have come to think of the database as more than just housing for the data. It really is the central point between the workflow tasks of design, development, and data. Designers, developers, and content editors all work with the variable data and templates tied together by the data-entry tool for entering content, previewing templates, and final production. The processes are streamlined, the data is clean, and the time-to-market for production of Flash movies is made easier, all because data is collected, organized, and distributed through the data-entry tool. And now that the data-entry tool is complete, you can move right into that final production phase. You have seen all three components of design, development, and content and their related workflow processes: the template, the database, and the data-entry tool. All that's left to do is to bring it all together and crank out the site

This chapter discussed the importance of clean and clear data entry. It also took you through the construction of a data-entry Web application. If you have gone through the chapters in this book chronologically, at this point in the workflow process you should have a complete understanding of site planning and the construction of the three main elements (the database, the template, and the data-entry tool). In the next chapter, all those pieces come together in the final production.

CHAPTER 6

Final Production: Putting All the Pieces Together

Where has all the time gone? It seems like only a short time ago that you came up with the brilliant idea of creating a dynamic Flash employee site. You have spent appropriate time in planning, built the database, created a solid design and template, and finally constructed the data-entry tool. In addition, it just so happens that everyone on your team has completed entering his or her own specific content (data) using the data-entry tool. And although everyone else was taking care of that, you moved ahead and created the static Main Navigation page. That was very smart and efficient of you!

Now that all the pieces are in place, it is just a matter of assembling them into a total site. First, you use the data-entry tool to actually process the Generator templates with the Generator server to create all the final Flash movies (SWF) and at the same time, all supporting HTML files too! Then you close up any loose holes and, tada, the complete employee site is ready for Big International Company. Before you do, however, remember to test like there's no tomorrow before shipping out the finished site. Take a deep breath. It is crunch time. Let's get to work!

This chapter covers the final step in the six-step workflow process using offline Generator. In particular, this chapter covers the following topics:

- Incorporating design, development, and content
- Processing templates with Generator
- Creating the supporting HTML files
- Testing and debugging
- Deploying the finished site
- Updating content in the future

Generating Flash Movies

Ahhh, the lore of crunch time—the period in the life cycle of every project that designers and developers both love and hate. Weeks, sometimes months of work culminate in this final phase of development. You are suddenly hit with the daunting task of assembling all the pieces into a concise and meaningful package at the eleventh hour. All the while, you make desperate attempts to keep tabs on your budget and the delivery deadline. And finally, you need to test like there's no tomorrow, and also make any last-minute corrections and changes (hopefully, not too many). It is all sometimes too overwhelming to think about. But rest easy my friend. Actually, with the proper planning and work you have already completed, the process of generating templates should be a breeze. The toughest part will be running through the entire site and making sure all the pieces work properly together.

Here's the game plan. You move the templates onto your personal Web server. Then, in the same manner that you built the testing functionality in the data-entry tool, you develop Generator processing functionality as well. First, you see how Generator processing happens with command-line processing. This will give you an understanding of Generator processing execution. With this in hand, you incorporate these same commands in the data-entry tool, using a third-party component to enhance the functionality of your ASP scripting.

The Goals of the Final Production

The number-one goal in this last part of the workflow process is to automate the processing of Generator templates in the data-entry tool. In a bit, you will see how traditional offline processing occurs by running Generator directly from the MS-DOS command line in Windows. Although you could automate the Generator command-line processing into a batch process, this chapter takes that thinking to the next level. By incorporating Generator processing into the data-entry tool, you have essentially created a one-stop-shop for dynamic content creation with Generator and Flash. This scripting environment will not only enable you to automate Generator processing in a single click, but you also will be able to do it faster and more reliably as well. Most importantly, however, the tool you have created is robust, open, and scalable. So as your site features grow and become more complex, so will your tools for Generator/Flash offline development.

Step 6: Generating the Site

Before you jump into processing, you must complete a few steps. First, make sure everything is in place. This is very important because the automated process in the data-entry tool requires that all files be present on the server. Make a quick check to see whether your templates and all external media (images) are in the proper locations on the server. (See Figure 6.1.)

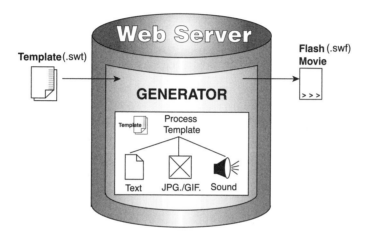

FIGURE 6.1   *The Generator process swaps variable content with real data from external files (such as text, images, and sound) and creates the resulting SWF file.*

Remember from Chapter 5, "The Data-Entry Tool," that the data-entry tool also required images to be stored in fixed locations. When employees entered the filename of their image in the data-entry tool, they also had to upload that image to a specified image directory on the server. The data-entry tool was smart enough to recognize when an image was properly stored by using the image filename entered. Referencing the image filename and seeing whether the file exists accomplished this task. When an employee first encounters the data-entry tool, a default image displays. When the image is properly uploaded to the server in the specified image directory, the employee's smiling face correctly displays in the data-entry tool. This quickly gives you a visual clue when an image is properly stored in the correct location, and Generator processing can proceed.

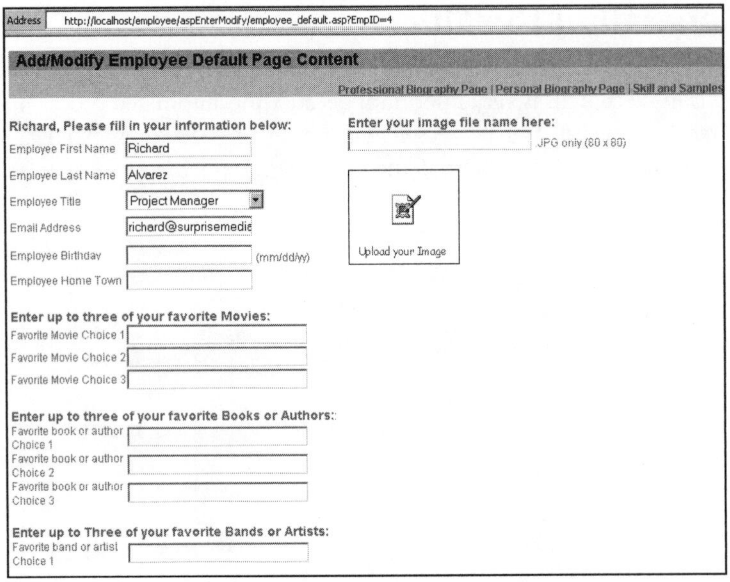

FIGURE 6.2   *The data-entry tool starts out with a default image displayed.*

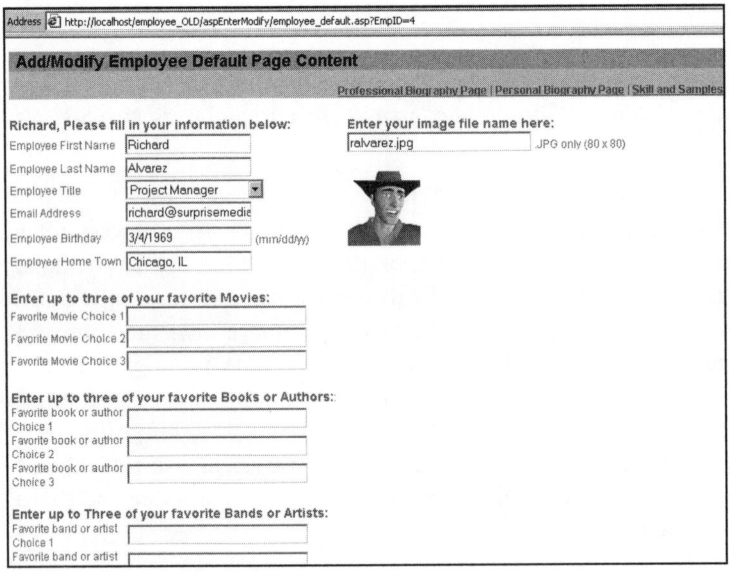

FIGURE 6.3   *This image of a well-mannered employee shows that the image was properly uploaded to the specified directory on the server. Let the Generator processing begin!*

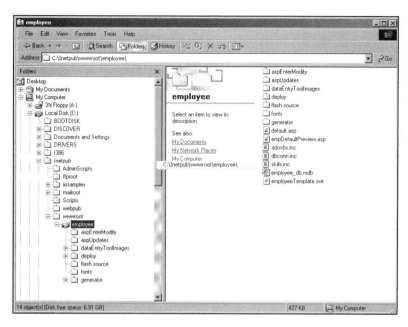

FIGURE 6.4   *The directory structure used in the employee site using offline Generator production workflow.*

Now that everything checks out, let's start processing.

Processing Templates with Generator

For the purpose of creating the employee site, offline Generator processing differs distinctly from online processing in a few specific ways. Offline Generator does not run as an extension of your Web server; instead, it is executed directly by invoking GENERATE.EXE. Also, offline Generator directly outputs a Flash movie on the server, whereas online Generator outputs a Flash movie to the client browser.

Essentially, with offline Generator processing, the keys to dynamic content are in your hands. You decide when and which templates are ready for Generator processing. You can update as often as you like, whenever you like. Then, post your finished FLAs on the server. The final results your site visitors will see are regular old Flash files. There's nothing special about that or the HTML files that package them either—just your standard <OBJECT>/<EMBED> tags. The following are the standard HTML <OBJECT><EMBED> tags for displaying Flash content in the browser:

```
<OBJECT CLASSID="clsid:D27CDB6E-AE6D-11cf-96B8-444553540000" WIDTH="760"
HEIGHT="18" CODEBASE="http://active.macromedia.com/flash5/cabs/
swflash.cab#version=5,0,0,0">
<PARAM NAME="MOVIE" VALUE="sample.swf">
<PARAM NAME="LOOP" VALUE="FALSE">
<PARAM NAME="QUALITY" VALUE="HIGH">
<PARAM NAME="SCALE" VALUE="EXACTFIT">

<EMBED SRC="sample.swf" WIDTH="760" HEIGHT="18"
LOOP="FALSE" QUALITY="HIGH" SCALE="EXACTFIT"
PLUGINSPAGE="http://www.macromedia.com/shockwave/download/
index.cgi?P1_Prod_
Version=ShockwaveFlash">
</EMBED>

</OBJECT>
```

Later you will see how the tools you build will create the supporting HTML as well (as just shown). Before you get into that, however, there's the task of producing the Flash movies. So take a look at traditional offline Generator processing invoked with the command-line executable.

> **note**
>
> **Generator Directory.** Before you start command-line processing with Generator, make sure that you are in the Generator directory on your system. In a Windows environment, Macromedia Generator typically installs to C:\ProgramFiles\Macromedia \Generator. As an alternative, you also could set your system path to include the Generator directory.

Command-Line Publishing

It is hard to believe that MS-DOS was the dominant operating system of choice for a time. It is even harder to believe that people actually remembered the correct syntax to type and get work done. Kudos to all our UNIX friends!

The following table lists offline Generator command-line output options.

Table 6.1   Generator Command-Line Output Options

Command	Result
-help	Displays descriptions of Generator options.
-swf *<FILENAME.SWF>*	Creates a Flash movie for output.
-gif *<FILENAME.GIF>*	Creates a GIF image for output.
-png *<FILENAME.PNG>*	Creates a PNG image for output.
-qtm *<FILENAME.MOV>*	Creates a QuickTime 4.0 movie for output.
-jpg *<FILENAME.JPG>*	Creates a JPEG image for output.
-txt *<FILENAME.TXT>*	Creates a text file from all the text within the movie.

Command	Result
-smap *<FILENAME*.MAP>	Creates a server-side image map.
-cmap *<FILENAME*.MAP>	Creates a client-side image map.
-cmapname *<name>*	Sets the client-side image map tag name.
-xwin32 *<FILENAME*.EXE>	Creates a Win32 projector.
-xmacppc <FILENAME.HQX>	Creates a Mac PPC projector.
-debug <1|2|3>	Specifies the level of detail you would like displayed in the log file. 1 displays only errors in the log file; 2 displays errors and warnings; 3 displays errors, warnings, and all data sources. You can specify the name of the log file using the -log option.
-log *<FILENAME*.TXT>	Specifies the log filename.
-param *<name>* <value>	Specifies a named parameter.
-font <path>	Specifies the path to search for external fonts.

To generate a Flash movie, you just use the –swf option shown in the preceding table. Basically, you need to invoke the generate command, an output option and its parameters, and the template. Below is the command-line syntax to create a Flash movie named SAMPLE.SWF from a template named SAMPLE.SWT.

```
c:> generate -swf MOVIE.SWF MOVIE.SWT
```

As is the case in the employee site that you are building, Flash movies are to be saved to a separate directory, whereas templates are located in another. You want to output the final Flash movies into a directory named Deploy. The templates are located in a directory named flash source. The modified command-line below shows how to generate the template.

```
c:> generate -swf C:\inetpub\wwwroot\Deploy\MOVIE.SWF
C:\inetpub\wwwroot\Source_Templates\MOVIE.SWT
```

That's pretty much it. Yes, it's true, there are many more options and parameters that you might use depending on the output you're looking for. Refer to Appendix A, "ActionScript for the Employee Navigation Main Screen," for additional information on setting offline Generator options. For the development of the employee site, this is enough to go on. Now, all that is left to do is to take basic functionality of offline command-line Generator processing and build it into the data-entry tool.

note

Exact Paths. The paths to the output directory and templates shown here are exact paths, where C:\ is the server drive. You also could use relative paths that are relative to the Generator directory.

Server-Scripted Publishing

First things first, however, before we get into the code. To begin, you want to insert a Generate button in the data-entry tool next to the Update button (as shown in Figure 6.5). This will be the Generator processing launch pad that will set the wheels of automated template generating in motion. The following code fragment not only displays the button, it also starts the Generator/Flash magic when clicked.

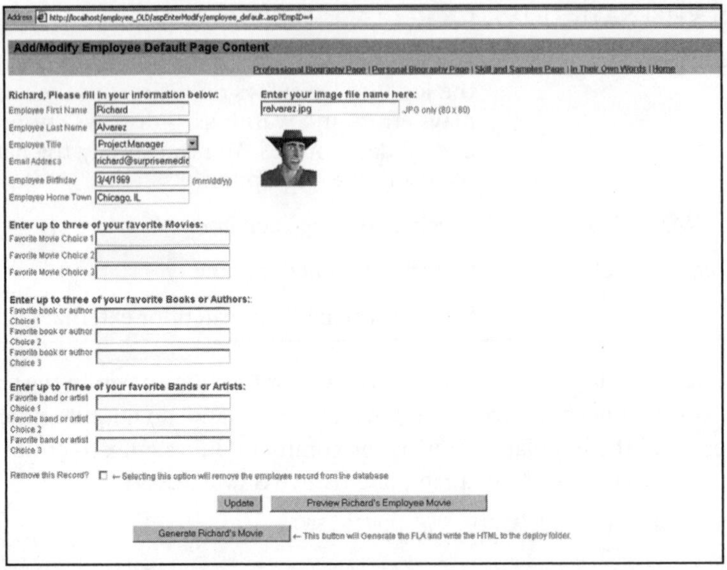

Figure 6.5   *Single-click Generator processing built into the data-entry tool.*

```
<input type="button" name="generate" value="Generate <%= RS("first_name")
%>'s Movie" onClick="window.location='../generator/makeSwf.asp?SWFName=<%=
RS("employee_ID") %>_employee.swf&SWTName=employeeTemplate.swt&EmpID=<%=
RS("employee_ID") %>&Parameter=empID&Value=<%= RS("employee_ID") %>'">
```

Wow. That is quite a bit to swallow all at once. If you break it down and do not get bogged down by the inserted ASP scripting, you will notice that it is really not that bad. Let's take it apart to see exactly what is going on.

This first part is easy. You are just inserting a form field button type.

```
<input type="button"
```

The next section is the value or name the button will display. In this case, you want the button to read Generate *Employee*'s Movie, where *Employee* is the first name of the current employee page being viewed in the data-entry tool. Recall from Chapter 5 that the record set (RS) holds the values returned from the SQL query. When IIS processes the ASP, it executes any script commands contained in the file and outputs a plain HTML Web page with the actual RS values inserted in the appropriate places. Just like that, every data-entry page is personalized. How nice.

```
value="Generate <%= RS("First_name") %>'s Employee Default Page"
```

And then there's the rest of the code. Whoa. This looks pretty scary; but again, it is not as bas as it looks.

```
onClick="window.location='../generator/makeSwf.asp?SWFName=<%=
RS("employee_ID")%>_employee.swf&SWTName=employeeTemplate.swt&EmpID=<%=
RS("employee_ID")%>&Parameter=empID&Value=<%= RS("employee_ID") %>'">
```

First, notice the onClick=. This is a standard DHTML event. The onClick event is used to execute script and/or functions when the user clicks a particular element, such as the newly inserted Generate button. In this case, what the Generate button will do is redirect the browser to a specific page, GEN_MAKE_SWF.ASP. The rest of the code is a list of parameters that you are passing to the GEN_MAKE_SWF.ASP page (four, to be exact). Table 6.2 lists each of the passed parameters and values separately.

Table 6.2

Parameter	Value - (Example)	Interpreted Value
SWFName	<%= RS("employee_ID") %>_empDefault.swf	(10_empDefault.swf)
SWTName	empDefault.swt	EmpDefault.swt
Parameter	EmpID	EmpID
Value	<% RS("employee_ID") %>	(10)

Each of these parameters are used in the GEN_MAKE_SWF.ASP page, as you are about to see.

As stated earlier, you will use a third-party component to extend the functionality of ASP. There is a freeware component provided by ServerObjects, Inc. at **www.serverobjects.com/products.htm** called ASPExec. With this handy little component, you can write an ASP page that enables you to execute DOS and Windows command applications in your ASP page. Sound familiar? Before you can use the

note

Browser Compatibility. The onClick event is supported by some versions of Netscape and older versions of Internet Explorer. Be sure that your development environment is using the required browser and version.

ASPExec component, however, you need to install the ASPExec component. This means registering the component ASPEXEC.DLL on your server.

Begin by moving the ASPEXEC.DLL file into a subdirectory on your server (for example, \Winnt\System32 for Windows NT or \Windows\System for Windows 95). Next, click Start and select Run. To register the component on the system, change to the directory where you installed the DLL and type the following:

```
regsvr32 ASPEXEC.DLL
```

> **note**
>
> **Make It Work.** To use this component if you run IIS as a service, go into Control Panel/Services/World Wide Web Publishing Service and turn on Allow Service to Interact with Desktop.

That is it. Now all you need to do is create the ASP page to execute the Generator command line. Before doing so, make sure that users will have proper execute access privileges on the server. After you have verified that all users have the proper read/write privileges to employee directories on the server, you are ready to proceed. You will create an instance of the object on the page using CreateObject(). Then build the parameters for the newly created instance of the object. Next, call the Execute method. Finally, redirect the browser to view the newly created Flash movie.

property Application	Set the path (optional) to an EXE/COM filename.
property Parameters	Set the application parameters.
property TimeOut	Set the timeout to wait (milliseconds). Used only for ExecuteDosApp and ExecuteWinAppAndWait.
property ShowWindow	Set whether the executing application is visible. Used only for ExecuteWinAppAndWait and ExecuteWinApp.
ExecuteDosApp	Executes the specified application as a DOS application and returns stdio as string.
ExecuteWinAppAndWait	Executes the specified application as a Windows application and waits for the specified timeout if execution is successful.
ExecuteWinApp	Executes the specified application as a Windows application and returns result code immediately.

Enough discussion on what you need to do, let's jump right into the code and do it! The following is GEN_MAKE_SWF.ASP deconstructed:

```
<%
' Create the server-side instance of the object
SET Executor = Server.CreateObject("ASPExec.Execute")
```

```
' Set the application name
Executor.Application = "c:\program files\macromedia\generator
2\generate.exe"
' Now, build the parameters to pass to the executing application
DIM Params
Params = "-swf c:\Inetpub\wwwroot\employee\deploy\" & Request("SWFName")
Params = Params & "-param " & Request("Parameter") & " " &
Request("Value") & " "
Params = Params & "c:\Inetpub\wwwroot\employee\" & Request("SWTName")
Executor.Parameters = Params
' Hide the Generator execution
Executor.ShowWindow = False
' Define a timeout length to allow Generator command-line execution
enough time to do its job
Executor.TimeOut = 10000
' Here's where you execute Generator. Output the result into a string
named intResult for verification of success
intResult = Executor.ExecuteWinAppAndWait
IF intResult = 258 then
    ' This is the result you want!
    strResult = "Execution successful"
ELSE
    '  Results of this method are the results of GetLastError
    strResult = "The result of this call was: " & intResult
END IF
' Redirect the browser to show it the newly generated Flash movie
RESPONSE.REDIRECT "../empDefaultPreview.asp?SWTName=" & Request
("SWTName") & ".swt&Parameter=" & Request("Parameter") & "&Value=" &
Request("IDValue")
%>
```

The first few lines are standard ASP conventions for using components and creating server-side objects. The main action occurs in building your parameter list to pass to Generator.

```
DIM Params
Params = "-swf c:\Inetpub\wwwroot\Employee\Deploy\" & Request("SWFName")
Params = Params & "-param " & Request("Parameter") & " " &
Request("Value") & " "
Params = Params & "c:\Inetpub\wwwroot\Employee\" & Request("SWTName")
```

It just so happens that the parameter list that you will pass to Generator, the executing application, is quite long. Recall from the discussion on command-line processing the syntax to generate a Flash movie. You also may have noticed that the ASP code includes a –param option that enables you to pass the template a parameter and value. The simplified code would look like this if you were typing it in as a command-line process:

```
generate –swf MOVIE.SWF –param value MOVIE.SWT
```

The `Params` variable construction begins by defining a variable you will use to store the string value of the parameter list you are about to build.

The first line of the `Params` build starts by creating a string containing the `-swf` option and the name you want to give to your new Flash movie. Remember that the Generate button on the data-entry tool not only called the GEN_MAKE_SWF.ASP page, but also passed it certain variables and values, including the name of the SWF file being generated.

```
DIM Params
Params = "-swf
c:\Inetpub\wwwroot\Employee\Deploy\" &
Request("SWFName")
```

The next line builds on the `Params` variable string by adding the `-param` option, parameter name, and value.

```
Params = Params & "-param " & Request("Parameter") & " " &
Request("Value") & " "
```

The last line in the `Params` construction adds the path to the template.

```
Params = Params & "c:\Inetpub\wwwroot\Employee\" & Request("SWTName")
```

If the Generate button on the data-entry tool passed the following parameters and values to the GEN_MAKE_SWF.ASP page

```
<input type="button" value="View Richard's Employee Default
Page"onclick="location='gen_make_swf.asp?SWFName=10_empDefault.swf&SWTNa
me=empDefault.swt&Parameter=empID&Value=10">
```

Here is what the `Params` variable would look like after being constructed by the GEN_MAKE_SWF.ASP page with the following parameters:

```
Params = -swf c:\Inetpub\wwwroot\Employee\Deploy\10_empDefault.swf -
param empID 10 c:\Inetpub\wwwroot\Employee\empDefault.swt
```

Now that that is built, you can proceed with the Generator execution. First, hide the actual command-line process from showing.

```
' Hide the Generator execution
Executor.ShowWindow = False
```

Because this entire offline process is being executed through the browser through a server request, you want to build in a wait cycle to give Generator enough time to complete before displaying the results. The timeout value is evaluated in milliseconds.

Therefore, a value of 10,000 equals 10 seconds. Next, you execute Generator and set the result to `intResult`. This way you can verify whether the execution succeeded. If it is not, you can return a value that can help you debug it if it did not succeed. Basically, a value of 258 is what you are looking for. Executing an application with an ASP component returns a value. If the value is not 258, you can verify where execution failed by checking the error code value that was returned.

```
' Define a timeout length to allow Generator command-line execution
enough time to do its job
Executor.TimeOut = 10000
' Here's where you execute Generator. Output the result into a string
named intResult for verification of success
intResult = Executor.ExecuteWinAppAndWait
IF intResult = 258 then
    ' This is the result you want!
    strResult = "Execution successful"
ELSE
    '  results of this method are the results of GetLastError
    strResult = "The result of this call was: " & intResult
    response.write ("Execution failed. Error: " & strResult)
END IF
```

Now that the Flash movie has been generated, you can redirect the browser to a page that will display it. The empDefaultPreview.asp page has pretty much the same ASP and HTML code as the template preview code you saw in Chapter 5.

```
' Redirect the browser to show it the newly generated Flash movie
RESPONSE.REDIRECT "empDefaultPreview.asp?SWTName=" & Request("SWTName")
& "&Parameter=" & Request("Parameter") & "&Value=" & Request("IDValue")
```

Here's the empDefaultPreview.asp page.

```
<HTML><HEAD><TITLE><%= Request("SWFName") %></TITLE></HEAD>
<BODY>

<OBJECT CLASSID="clsid:D27CDB6E-AE6D-11cf-96B8-444553540000"
WIDTH="760"
HEIGHT="450"
CODEBASE="http://active.macromedia.com/flash5/cabs/swflash.cab#version=
5,0,0
,0" ID="check">
    <PARAM NAME=MOVIE VALUE="<%= Request("SWTName") %>?<%=
Request("Parameter") %>=<%= Request("Value") %>">
    <PARAM NAME=QUALITY VALUE="HIGH">
    <PARAM NAME=MENU VALUE="FALSE">
    <PARAM NAME=SALIGN VALUE="C">
    <PARAM NAME=BGCOLOR VALUE="#336666">

<EMBED SRC="<%= Request("SWTName") %>?<%= Request("Parameter") %>=<%=
Request("Value") %>"
 swLiveConnect="FALSE" WIDTH="760" HEIGHT="420" QUALITY="HIGH"
```

continues

Continued

```
MENU="FALSE"
BGCOLOR="#336666" SALIGN="C" TYPE="application/x-shockwave-flash"
PLUGINSPAGE="http://www.macromedia.com/shockwave/download/
index.cgi?P1_Prod_
Version=ShockwaveFlash">
</EMBED>

</OBJECT>

</BODY>
</HTML>
```

There's really no new scripting in the empDefaultPreview.asp page. As you have seen before, you just inserted ASP scripting values for the page title and SRC value in the <OBJECTS> and <EMBED> tags. Again, when this ASP page is processed by IIS, the page is returned as plain HTML.

If there were only a way to create and save supporting HTML files, such as the preceding page, to the Deploy directory on the server, your work would be complete.

Supporting HTML

The code that follows writes the necessary Flash HTML wrapper using built-in methods included in ASPs. For this task, you use the ASP file-access component, which gives you all the basic ways to work with the file system (for example, to create and write a file to the server). Wouldn't that just be incredibly convenient?

Of course, the file-access object offers nearly a hundred different ways to manipulate the file system (far beyond the scope of this chapter). Refer to Appendix A for additional information and resources for ASP development. For now, the following code will cover your needs for automating the Generator process.

Without further ado, on to the code. Ladies and gentlemen, aspWriteHtml.asp.

```
' The WriteToFile function takes a path and text string as parameters

FUNCTION WriteToFile(filename, filecontent)
  SET objFSO = CreateObject("Scripting.FileSystemObject")
  SET objFile = objFSO.CreateTextFile(filename)
  ObjFile.Write(filecontent)
  ObjFile.Close
END FUNCTION

FileString = "<HTML>" & vbcrlf & "<HEAD><TITLE>" & Request("EmpID") &
"_empDefault Page</TITLE>" & vbcrlf & "</HEAD>" & vbcrlf & "<BODY>" &
vbcrlf
FileString = FileString & "<OBJECT classid=" &
"""clsid:D27CDB6E-AE6D-11cf-96B8-444553540000" & """ codebase=" &
```

```
"""http://active.macromedia.com/flash5/cabs/
swflash.cab#version=5,0,0,0" & """ ID=check WIDTH=760 HEIGHT=420>" &
vbcrlf
FileString = FileString & "<PARAM NAME=movie VALUE=""" &
Request("EmpID") &
"_empDefault.swf"">"  & vbcrlf
FileString = FileString & "<PARAM NAME=quality VALUE=high>" & vbcrlf
FileString = FileString & "<PARAM NAME=menu VALUE=false>" & vbcrlf
FileString = FileString & "<PARAM NAME=salign VALUE=C>" & vbcrlf
FileString = FileString & "<PARAM NAME=bgcolor VALUE=#336666>"  & vbcrlf
FileString = FileString & "<EMBED SRC=""" & Request("EmpID") &
"_empDefault.swf"" swLiveConnect=FALSE WIDTH=760 HEIGHT=420 QUALITY=high
MENU=false BGCOLOR=#336666 SALIGN=C TYPE=" &
"""application/x-shockwave-flash" & """ PLUGINSPAGE=" &
"""http://www.macromedia.com/shockwave/download/index.cgi?P1_Prod_
Version=ShockwaveFlash" & """>" & vbcrlf
FileString = FileString & "</EMBED>" & vbcrlf & "</OBJECT>" & vbcrlf &
"</BODY></HTML>"

' write the file using the WriteToFile function defined above
Call WriteToFile(Server.MapPath("deploy/" & Request("EmpID") &
"_empDefault.html"), FileString)

%>
```

Again, as in the GEN_MAKE_SWF.ASP page, the heart of the code is in constructing the FileString. This is the very content of the HTML wrapper page. As you may have noticed, the preceding code splits the construction of FileString into nine separate lines of code. In actuality, the same assignment could have occurred in a single line of code. It was broken up this way for clarity and for simpler debugging.

You also might notice that the actual text writing was built as a function. In this way, you can include this code as part of the GEN_MAKE_SWF.ASP page. The function takes two parameters: a filename, including its path; and the contents to write to the file. The WriteToFile function is made up of four simple and direct lines of code. Those four lines of code perform the following actions:

> **note**
>
> **Hard Return.** Use vbcrlf to force a hard carriage return in your newly created HTML file.

Create an instance of the FileSystemObject.

Create a file with the filename passed to the WriteToFile function.

Write the contents passed to the WriteToFile function into the newly create file.

Close the instance of the FileSystemObject.

The next nine lines in the aspWriteHtml.asp are dedicated to building the contents of the new file. Starting from a Flash HTML wrapper file and pasting the source of that file into aspWriteHtml.asp page makes the creation of this code much easier. All you need to do is substitute the Flash movie names with ASP variable scripting. You also need to pay careful attention to the use of quotation marks. Basically, use multiple quotes ("") to display a set of quotation marks in your HTML.

The last line of code in aspWriteHtml.asp makes a call to the `WriteToFile` function. You pass it the name and path of the supporting HMTL for a specific Flash movie, and `FileString` (the string you just completed building).

If you made a call to aspWriteHtml.asp with the following parameters

```
aspWriteHtml.asp?empID=11&SWTName=empDefault.swt
```

Here's what the resulting HTML file would look like:

```
<HTML>
<HEAD><TITLE>11_empDefault Page</TITLE></HEAD>
<BODY>

<OBJECT classid="clsid:D27CDB6E-AE6D-11cf-96B8-444553540000"
codebase="http://active.macromedia.com/flash5/cabs/swflash.cab#version=
5,0,0
,0" ID=check WIDTH=760 HEIGHT=420>
<PARAM NAME=MOVIE VALUE="11_empDefault.swf">
<PARAM NAME=QUALITY VALUE="HIGH">
<PARAM NAME=MENU VALUE="FALSE">
<PARAM NAME=SALIGN VALUE="C">
<PARAM NAME=BGCOLOR VALUE="#336666">

<EMBED SRC="11_empDefault.swf" swLiveConnect=FALSE WIDTH="760"
HEIGHT="420"
QUALITY="HIGH" MENU="FALSE" BGCOLOR="#336666" SALIGN="C"
TYPE="application/x-shockwave-flash"
PLUGINSPAGE="http://www.macromedia.com/shockwave/download/index.cgi?P1_
Prod_
Version=ShockwaveFlash">
</EMBED>

</OBJECT>

</BODY></HTML>
```

Test, Test, and Test Again

You have just completed the Generator processing for the last employee content page. All the Flash movies and HTML files are properly organized in the Deploy directory.

That's the true beauty of the work you have just completed. The offline workflow process and the automated features you just built into the data-entry tool make deploying the employee site a breeze. It is all there in Deploy, and is ready for shipment.

Do not upload those files to your Web server just yet, however. After all the hard work put in over the past few weeks, now is not the time to rush and cut corners. No sir. It is time to roll up your sleeves and test the employee site. Better yet, get your friendly co-workers to lend some time to looking over the completed site. Site testing is a tedious and difficult task. The more eyes devoted to testing, the better.

If you are fortunate enough to have a Q/A team devoted to project testing, all the better. If not, take a page out of the Q/A book and develop a series of testing parameters of your own. Some must-test practices include browser and platform tests, system memory tests, and connection-speed tests.

Perhaps even invest some time and money in researching appropriate Web site management and testing tools. These can make your life so much easier with automated utilities that enable you to test the following:

- Web site security
- Stress and load testing
- Page load and performance
- Check for broken links
- HTML validation
- Browser and platform testing

In testing the entire site, try to see the whole as well as the pieces. Check for obvious and subtle things alike. Even if you do not have a Q/A team in place, or a suite of site management and testing tools, spend the time to run through the whole site and test for performance, functionality, and visual consistency and design.

System Checks

Verify that the HTML and client-side scripting is working properly. Again, be sure to do proper browser and platform checks. What happens when plug-in detection fails? Plan for it and provide proper detection failure workarounds. Give the user the option to download the proper plug-ins or view an alternative non-plug-in page.

Come up with your own brand of testing scenarios to perform the same type of checks listed in this section. For instance, split up responsibilities among the group. Have some testers check all the links. Have others look at the site on different browsers and platforms.

Visual Checks

Look to see how the pages fit together. Do the pages flow from one to the other as outlined in the storyboards? Motion graphics is all about timing. Look for visual as well as audio clues (if applicable), to test the timing of animations.

Check for placement of elements and spacing. Does your template allow enough room for variable content? Here is where your storyboards are worth their weight in gold. Dynamic content sometimes has a way of pushing other elements around. Your storyboards should have allowed for variable-sized data. If a visual error such as this occurs, the easiest solution is to tweak the content.

Finally, check the interactive elements in the site. Do all rollovers work properly? Are the different button states (up, down, rollover, disabled) functioning? Do they all do what they are supposed to do or go where they are supposed to go?

Deploying the Site

Testing the site takes on a cyclical pattern. You make your system and visual tests, make the necessary corrections, and test again. Keep running through that cycle until you come away feeling comfortable about deploying the site (or the budget is gone and the client's lawyers come to visit). In all seriousness, the amount of time and effort you put in to testing will greatly reward you in the long run. When your testing is complete, then and only then, are you ready to upload the contents of the Deploy folder onto your Web server.

That is really all there is to deploying the site. Everything needed, all Flash SWF movies, supporting HTML files, and external media are neatly stored and organized in the Deploy directory.

Timed Updates

So now that the site has been tested, posted on the server, and is in perfect shape, the job is done and you come out looking like a genius. And because updates can be easily accomplished, the employee site is always current. Whether hourly, daily, or monthly, the offline Generator workflow process is up to the challenge. That is the essence of offline Generator.

In fact, if you knew that content updates needed to be made on a regular basis, you could run scripted batch files to perform the processing and posting of newly created Flash movies on your site. Macromedia explains this process in a white paper titled ASPGenIntegration. Refer to **www.macromedia.com** for further information on scheduling timed updates with ASP and Generator.

Chapter Summary

In this chapter, you explored the following topics:

- **Generating the site.** The final step in the workflow process for offline Generator is the incorporation of design, development, and content. You used the data-entry tool to process the templates with Generator, as well as to create all supporting HTML files.

- **Testing.** Your work is not complete until you have done some testing. At the very least, you should do a quick run through the entire site to test for any visual, functional, and/or site flow mistakes.

- **Updates.** Using the techniques you learned in creating the employee site, it is just as easy to keep the content fresh and up to date as well.

Big International Company was very impressed with the work and processes involved at your firm. The employee site was received with a standing ovation by the big shot at Big International Company, who went as far as to say, "I feel like I personally know each and every one of the great employees in your firm, and it's all due to that awesome employee site!" Honestly, she really did say that. Okay, maybe she did not use the word *awesome*. The point is they loved it. More importantly, you gained the knowledge and tools to build a Web application for producing incredible Flash content sites using offline Generator. Whereas most other team members completed weeks and months of design and development on other projects, you put an entire 250+ page site together in about three weeks!

As current employee data changed and new employees came onboard, keeping the site current was a simple click of the mouse. Generator processing and HTML files were created all at once, instantly. All you needed to do after that was select the newly created files and upload them to the Web server. Because the process of updating pages was so simple, even your manager could generate a new movie and post the files.

You could end this story here with a simple, "they all lived happily ever after." But why? Now that you have seen how design and development can use Generator and Flash to build great dynamic sites, the stories are just about to begin!

CHAPTER 7

Conclusion

Your work with offline Generator is now complete. In the whirlwind of design and development, however, what actually happened? More importantly, how can you build from the experience of developing the mock employee site? This chapter retraces the steps of the workflow process described in detail throughout the preceding six chapters. This chapter revisits each step so that you will understand its place in the workflow. It then explains how you can use the knowledge and tools used in the employee project to build your next Generator project.

In particular, this chapter covers the following topics:

- Reviewing each step of the workflow process for a final thought.
- Providing common practices and tips from real-world site development.
- Discussing the integration of the steps in the Generator workflow.
- Learning how to use the concepts from the workflow process to build automated tools for site development.
- Building from the ideas of offline Generator mode to deliver with online Generator.
- Communicating and storytelling with content-driven sites.

Big International Company was so impressed with the work and the workflow process involved at your firm that the big shot herself was quoted as saying, "I feel like I know everyone on your team personally." While everyone else in your firm completed weeks and months of design and development on other projects, you put an entire 250+ page inter-active site together in about three weeks! Not only did your firm get the huge Big International Company account, but you also got a big fat raise, time off to relax somewhere warm, and the respect and admiration of everyone on your team! So where do you go from here? (That is, after you get back all nice and tanned, of course.) You could begin by breaking down the many techniques used to build the employee site for specialized automated processes in your organization. Perhaps you could take a stab at bringing the employee site project to the next level and make it truly dynamic, utilizing Macromedia Generator online mode. Or, you could take everything you have learned and work on the next great site. This chapter wraps up the six steps in the workflow process, and then attempts to reach beyond what was covered here and to build on it.

Review: The Workflow Process

Well there you have it, the workflow process for building dynamic sites with Generator and Flash, quickly and efficiently. You now have a complete knowledge of offline Generator development and the workflow process to use as a model for building dynamic, database-driven Flash sites for e-commerce, training, and storytelling productions.

1. Brainstorming
2. Storyboarding the Site
3. Building the Database
4. Designing the Template
5. Creating a Data-Entry Tool
6. Generating the Site

"How did this workflow process come about?" you ask. Actually, the steps created themselves. After numerous attempts to create offline sites, you stick with the practices that work and modify the ones that do not. After multiple passes, you learn from your mistakes and add improvements and the required planning and testing that naturally accompanies all your projects. When you do so, you end up with the six steps in the workflow process.

Central to the workflow process are the three key ingredients: the database, the template, and the data-entry tool. It is obvious that Generator development requires a template. In fact, the basic definition of Generator development is creating a Flash movie with variable elements and saving it as a template file. The database and data-entry tool are really optional.

The necessary data source, as you learned, can come from various sources, including a comma-delimited text file, a URL that references a comma-delimited text file, a result set from a SQL query padded through JDBC/ODBC connection, or a Java class. The workflow process used a database and the data-entry tool as the mechanism for storing and accessing data, and for Generator processing.

These three key ingredients work together to create an optimal procedure for orchestrating the disciplines of design, development, and content editing simultaneously. They enable you to work from a single template design. This single template enables you to produce multiple Flash movies with consistent design and flow, a single database to house and manage relational content, and finally, a single data-entry tool to administer content input and Generator processing.

Let's review the six individual steps in the workflow process one last time.

Step 1: Brainstorming

Every great idea starts somewhere. Regardless of how the initial thought came to light, it needs to be polished and developed. Do not be fooled into thinking that brainstorming sessions just happen on their own. Spend allocated project time to perform good brainstorming sessions with your team.

Another important thing to consider is involving various team members. Do not limit brainstorming sessions to just the same creative folks in design. Invite programmers, project managers, content editors, and whoever else is willing to spend time refining strong ideas. Variety really is the spice of life, and it could not be truer than in brainstorming (especially the variety from cross-disciplines involved in the project, such as development, content editing, and project management). The more angles you cover, the stronger your design will be; the time spent thinking through all possibilities will cross into all related steps in the workflow process.

Although it is true that larger, diverse teams make for stronger brainstorming sessions, be careful not to turn your brainstorming sessions into chaotic nonproductive sessions. Sometimes you may have too many individuals involved in the brainstorming sessions. You may have too many people in your brainstorming sessions if your meetings separate into diverse groups discussing separate ideas. Another indication of too many "cooks in the kitchen" is when the atmosphere is unorganized and individuals forget the purpose of the meetings.

This is not to say that you want to avoid unrelated thoughts that clash. Shoot for every angle, good and bad. Remember from Chapter 1, "Planning Production Before Production," the goal of every brainstorming meeting is not to nail down the exact design and site elements. Instead, the goal is to ask and answer the following questions:

- Who is the audience?
- What are the elements that will make up the site?
- What is the general flow of the site?

1. Main Navigation

2. Employee Default Page

3. Professional Biography

4. Personal Biography

5. Skills and Samples

6. In Their Own Words

If you can come away with just those questions answered, consider the brainstorming session a success. Chances are that you will come away with much more. If nothing else, important decisions such as directions and elements to avoid are almost a certain result.

Step 2: Storyboarding the Site

In Chapter 2, "Designing Beyond Look and Feel," you built on the brainstorming session by adding definition and exact order, placement, flow, and design. The storyboards and wire-frames, like the one pictured in Figure 7.1, were used throughout the remaining steps as a guide to building the mock employee site. They gave your team of designers and developers vital instructions about what would happen, how it would happen, and the content that needed to be developed to make it happen.

Employee Template Movie/Initial Scene

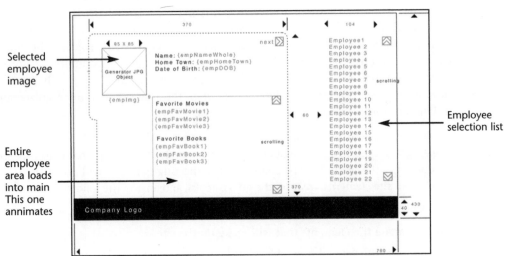

FIGURE 7.1   *Example of storyboards used in the employee site.*

You create storyboards to visualize the flow of the story. As you learned in Chapter 2, storyboards help in the problem-solving and planning stages by enabling you to ensure that all phases of development and design are covered. Consider the benefits of storyboarding described in the following list:

- Storyboarding helps you plan, produce, and evaluate.

- Storyboarding enables you to detail the makeup and structure of your project (and its component parts).

- Storyboarding forces you to organize your ideas.

- Storyboarding initiates the production of resources to be used in the project.

- Storyboarding gives you a rough visual representation of what the site will look like and how it will flow.

Step 3: Building the Database

The workflow process for rapid site development with Macromedia Generator and Flash centers around three main elements: the database, the template, and content. (See Figure 7.2.) In Chapter 3, "Developing the Database," you looked at the first of those three main elements: the database.

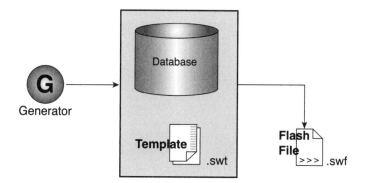

FIGURE 7.2   *The database houses the content and sits in the center of the workflow process.*

Yes, it is true: People spend thousands of dollars training to become certified experts at relational database-management systems such as Oracle, IBM DB2, Microsoft SQL Server, Sybase, and Informix. Chapter 3's discussion of databases broke down the technological mumbo-jumbo into simple objectives that almost everyone can perform. The database you used to build the mock employee site was Microsoft Access. Although not as robust as the database packages mentioned earlier, Access is very accessible to most, and it serves the needed functions to build the dynamic applications of the employee site.

The reason to create and set up the database is to house the content that will eventually populate the templates. As the keeper of the content, the database plays the following important roles:

- **Content management.** The database is a collection of data that is organized into tables, records, and fields. Although you could supply alternative data sources to Generator, without the database, it is very likely that you would have to keep track of the data from a variety of sources, organize, update/delete, and create data relationships on your own. (See Figure 7.3.)
- **Data sharing.** Data sharing enables you to share data with everyone involved in the process, including team members who enter and modify content that is placed in the database. Data sharing also includes workflow elements, such as the templates and the data-entry tool, that use the database as a data source for displaying content and generating processing.
- **Creating a data source.** Using a language called SQL, you can query, update, and manage your relational database. SQL enables you to retrieve, sort, and filter specific content from one or more tables using specific criteria you specify. (See Figure 7.4.)

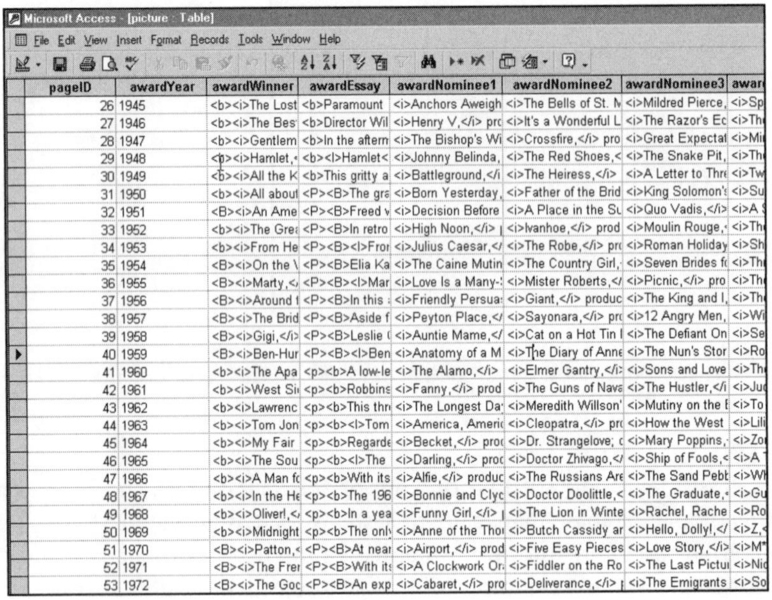

pageID	awardYear	awardWinner	awardEssay	awardNominee1	awardNominee2	awardNominee3	awar
26	1945	<b><i>The Lost	<b>Paramount	<i>Anchors Aweigh	<i>The Bells of St.	<i>Mildred Pierce,	<i>Sp
27	1946	<b><i>The Bes	<b>Director Wil	<i>Henry V,</i> pr	<i>It's a Wonderful L	<i>The Razor's Ec	<i>Th
28	1947	<b><i>Gentlem	<b>In the aftern	<i>The Bishop's Wi	<i>Crossfire,</i> pro	<i>Great Expecta	<i>Mi
29	1948	<b><i>Hamlet,	<b><I>Hamlet<	<i>Johnny Belinda,	<i>The Red Shoes,<	<i>The Snake Pit,	<i>Th
30	1949	<b><i>All the K	<b>This gritty a	<i>Battleground,</i	<i>The Heiress,</i>	<i>A Letter to Thr	<i>Tw
31	1950	<b><i>All about	<P><B>The gr	<i>Born Yesterday,	<i>Father of the Brid	<i>King Solomon'	<i>Su
32	1951	<B><i>An Ame	<P><B>Freed	<i>Decision Before	<i>A Place in the S	<i>Quo Vadis,</i>	<i>A
33	1952	<b><i>The Gre	<P><B>In retro	<i>High Noon,</i>	<i>Ivanhoe,</i> prod	<i>Moulin Rouge,	<i>Th
34	1953	<b><i>From He	<P><B><I>Fro	<i>Julius Caesar,</	<i>The Robe,</i> pr	<i>Roman Holiday	<i>Sh
35	1954	<B><i>On the	<P><B>Elia Ka	<i>The Caine Mutin	<i>The Country Girl,	<i>Seven Brides f	<i>Th
36	1955	<B><i>Marty,<	<P><B><I>Mar	<i>Love Is a Many-	<i>Mister Roberts,</	<i>Picnic,</i> pro	<i>Th
37	1956	<B><i>Around	<P><B>In this	<i>Friendly Persua	<i>Giant,</i> produc	<i>The King and I,	<i>Th
38	1957	<B><i>The Brid	<P><B>Aside f	<i>Peyton Place,</	<i>Sayonara,</i> pr	<i>12 Angry Men,	<i>Wi
39	1958	<B><i>Gigi,</i	<P><B>Leslie	<i>Auntie Mame,</	<i>Cat on a Hot Tin	<i>The Defiant On	<i>Se
40	1959	<B><i>Ben-Hur	<P><B><I>Ben	<i>Anatomy of a M	<i>The Diary of Ann	<i>The Nun's Stor	<i>Ro
41	1960	<b><i>The Apa	<p><b>A low-le	<i>The Alamo,</i>	<i>Elmer Gantry,</i	<i>Sons and Love	<i>Th
42	1961	<b><i>West Si	<p><b>Robbins	<i>Fanny,</i> prod	<i>The Guns of Nav	<i>The Hustler,</i	<i>Ju
43	1962	<b><i>Lawrenc	<p><b>This thr	<i>The Longest Da	<i>Meredith Willson'	<i>Mutiny on the	<i>To
44	1963	<b><i>Tom Jon	<p><b><I>Tom	<i>America, Ameri	<i>Cleopatra,</i> pr	<i>How the West	<i>Lili
45	1964	<b><i>My Fair	<p><b>Regard	<i>Becket,</i> pro	<i>Dr. Strangelove;	<i>Mary Poppins,	<i>Zo
46	1965	<b><i>The Sou	<p><b><I>The	<i>Darling,</i> pro	<i>Doctor Zhivago,</	<i>Ship of Fools,<	<i>A
47	1966	<b><i>A Man f	<p><b>With its	<i>Alfie,</i> produc	<i>The Russians Ar	<i>The Sand Peb	<i>W
48	1967	<b><i>In the H	<p><b>The 196	<i>Bonnie and Cly	<i>Doctor Doolittle,<	<i>The Graduate,	<i>Gu
49	1968	<b><i>Oliver!,<	<p><b>In a yea	<i>Funny Girl,</i>	<i>The Lion in Winte	<i>Rachel, Rache	<i>Ro
50	1969	<b><i>Midnight	<p><b>The onl	<i>Anne of the Tho	<i>Butch Cassidy ar	<i>Hello, Dolly!,</	<i>Z,
51	1970	<B><i>Patton,	<P><B>At nea	<i>Airport,</i> prod	<i>Five Easy Pieces	<i>Love Story,</i>	<i>M*
52	1971	<B><i>The Fre	<P><B>With it	<i>A Clockwork Or	<i>Fiddler on the Ro	<i>The Last Pictu	<i>Ni
53	1972	<B><i>The Go	<P><B>An exp	<i>Cabaret,</i> pro	<i>Deliverance,</i>	<i>The Emigrants	<i>So

FIGURE 7.3 *Databases, such as Microsoft Access, organize data through the use of tables, records, and fields.*

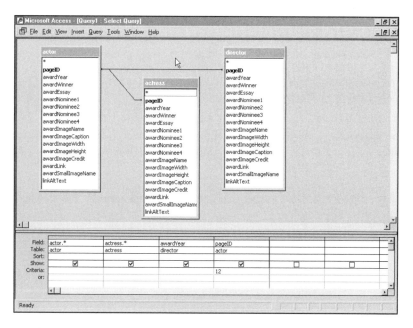

FIGURE 7.4   *Building a SQL query statement in Microsoft Access Query Design view.*

Step 4: Designing the Template

The second main element in the workflow process is the template. The templates contain placeholders for text, graphics, animations, sounds, charts, graphs, tables, and the rest of the Generator objects. Generator processes the template with content from a data source to create a Flash movie. Building off the storyboards created in Chapter 2, you fashioned a design to hold both static and dynamic elements.

The combination of static and dynamic elements formed a shell or template. Then, when supplied with a data source and processed with Generator, these elements were used to create each of the employee movies with unique content. You learned how to use Flash Generator objects that come with Generator Developer Studio as placeholders for dynamic content. You have various Generator objects to select from, depending on the type of content to be generated (including text, images, lists, and charts). Once the appropriate Generator object was selected, specific parameters set, and a data source supplied, you entered variable content in brackets. Then, when the SWT template was processed with Generator, the variable names were replaced with actual employee content.

In addition to converting your Flash movies into dynamic templates, the chapter showed you how to plan and design layered Flash movies, optimize their file size, and also showed you common Flash design standards and practices.

Step 5: Creating a Data-Entry Tool

The third and last element in the workflow process triangle is the data-entry tool. The data-entry tool, like the one shown in Figure 7.5, used Microsoft Active Server Pages scripting to perform insert, update, and delete functions on the data in the mock employee site database.

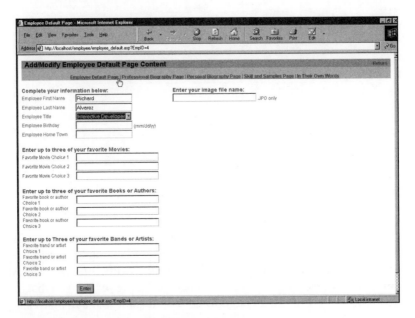

FIGURE 7.5   *A content entry page from the data-entry tool.*

As a central location for content entry, the data-entry tool served multiple roles. As a data-entry tool, it allowed the disciplines of design, development, and content to be created and refined independently. Employees had access to a Web interface application and their own content area.

After the data had been entered, it served as an important test bed for content error checking. Data could be entered, modified, and deleted over and over again. You also included shortcut data-entry techniques to ensure uniform and clean data entry (for example, radio buttons, drop-down lists, and automatic data selections).

You also implemented a template preview feature that allowed for testing design layout and flow. Designers could look at the finished template with real content and check for visual inconsistencies and/or areas within the template that did not hold up. Content editors could easily see how the data entered was displayed. If it was not to their liking, they could quickly modify and adjust the visual display on-the-fly.

Lastly, building off of the preview capabilities, the data-entry tool served as the final integration stage for Generator processing. Final Flash movies were created on demand and organized in a final production directory. All supporting HTML files were created and stored along with Flash movies.

The following list highlights the main benefits of the data-entry tool:

- A central location for entering and modifying data
- Template preview and testing for design and content
- Final integration of content and template for Generator processing

Step 6: Generating the Site

You dedicated appropriate time planning for the site with brainstorming sessions and preparing storyboards. You completed the construction of the database and the data-entry tool. And last, but not least, you devoted quality time to design in the development of the template.

Chapter 6, "Final Production: Putting All the Pieces Together," showed you how all of the following steps come together in the Generator processing of templates to movies. You saw how the data-entry tool was used to perform the final processing and packaging to deliver the site.

1. In the same manner that data was entered and displayed in the data-entry tool, you were able to request employee-specific data, format the result as a comma-delimited text file, and pass it on to the template.

2. You used a third-party ASP component to invoke the Generator command-line EXE to process templates into movies.

3. You saved the resulting SWF file in a deployment directory along with the supporting HTML files.

4. You performed your final checks and testing procedures of the final deployment directory.

5. After everything checked out A-OK, you and the employee site were golden. You moved the final deployment directory out to your Web server and waited for the praise to start pouring in!

Building On What We Have Built

When producing dynamic sites using Generator and templates, experience is obviously a major factor. The more the workflow is used, the more of an understanding of how the process works—its nuances, advantages, and so on. With this basic understanding will come a comfort level. Sometimes, however, when developing with Generator and Flash, the comfort level may not come as quickly or as smoothly as you may like. Deadlines, unknown functionality, guesswork, scope creep, and redesign are all factors that designers and developers must deal with daily. Knowing your tools and how to use them is an effective way to ease the transition.

While rolling smoothly, or not so smoothly along, there are practices that will develop. These standards usually come about because of supply and demand. Your client demands something, and usually you supply it. What they demand is not always what was originally asked. After numerous requests for nearly the same thing, however, you build up a small bag of tricks to ease the way and make your client a happy soul.

With these common tricks up your sleeve, you will notice that your workflow is smoother, your actual work is organized, and even a certain development or design style is acquired. Your art or development will be streamlined to keep up with the fastest of any development/design machines.

Style before function, function before style—it isn't just making art any more—it's building your functionality and getting into a manageable pattern with the workflow process steps.

Let's not gloss over the creation of the supporting HTML files that were produced when building the mock employee site. At the heart of the workflow process is the dynamic ability to change content on-the-fly and at your discretion. As this book has stressed all along, *content is king*! The workflow process treats the content in such a manner. Whether that means supplying content to templates processed through Generator offline (or online) to produce Flash Movies or even, yes, HTML. Content is what it is all about.

Hundreds of books focus on dynamic site development using server-side scripting (such as ASP). This book just gave you the "enough-to-be-dangerous" version. The techniques in Steps 1, 2, 3, and 5 of the workflow process remain the same. Step 4, "Designing the Template," in this case, would be replaced with the ASP template. The variable names in the HTML version are produced with ASP placeholders.

Refer to Appendix B, "Resources," for additional recommended readings on database and ASP site development.

note

Generator can also output a GIF, animated GIF, JPEG, PNG, QuickTime, Image Maps (client and server-side), and executable for the Macintosh and Windows platforms.

Online Generator

This book outlined a formula for rapid, dynamic site development using techniques for Generator processing in offline mode. As you learned in the Introduction, Generator can be developed in two distinct modes: offline and online.

The offline flavor that the workflow process was built on puts the actual Generator processing on you, the developer/designer. Through the functionality built in to the data-entry tool, you decide when and which templates are ready for Generator processing.

In the online mode, the Web server does the work of Generator processing. Whenever a site visitor comes across a page on your site with dynamic Flash content, Generator server delivers the real-time processing of that Flash movie.

Although it is true that the Developer Edition of Generator can accommodate your online processing needs, it is not made for heavy-traffic sites that require an abundant amount of Generator processing. Macromedia created the Developer Edition specifically for offline processing and infrequent online content updates.

To handle the high demand of Generator processing on your Web server, Macromedia created the Enterprise Edition of Generator. Generator 2 Enterprise Edition is a high-performance, scalable solution specifically engineered to deliver real-time dynamic content in Flash. Among its various technological highlights are its tremendous caching capabilities that enable your Web server to work smarter. Another important difference from the Developer Edition is its scalability. Generator 2 Enterprise Edition can scale across CPUs and servers. This feature gives Generator server the capability to accommodate thousands, even millions of visitors to your site with ease.

Therefore, although it is possible to develop online Generator with the Developer Edition of Generator, depending on the needs of your site, your best bet for online development is most likely Enterprise Edition.

Consider the following if you are planning to serve real-time content with Enterprise Edition:

- How large of a site do you plan to create with Generator content?
- What kind of traffic do you get on your site?
- Are there periods when many hits will be made to your site for the same page at the same time?
- Is your site infrastructure made up of multiple servers?
- Consider the cost of Generator 2 Enterprise Edition, which starts at $30,000 and increases based on usage.

Macromedia states that the real differences between the Enterprise and Developer Editions are in performance, scalability, and administration. Here's how they describe those differences on their Web site:

Performance. Enterprise Edition has caching technology, which stores frequently requested information for reuse on the Web site. By using the multi-level caching system, you can increase the performance of Generator 2 Enterprise Edition by anywhere from 30% to 200%. Developer Edition does not include caching.

Scalability. Enterprise Edition is multi-threaded. It scales to take advantage of additional processing power when more CPUs are added. Developer Edition is single-threaded. It does not scale across CPUs and does not take advantage of the additional processing power that more CPUs provide.

Administration. Enterprise Edition includes a browser based administration servlet for real-time administration. It allows you to set the caching levels, track the media delivered (SWF, GIF, JPG, PNG, QuickTime), and administer the server remotely. Developer Edition does not include any administration capabilities.

> **note**
>
> **Single- and Multi-Threaded.** To illustrate the difference between single- and multi-threaded functions, consider this example. You and five other drivers are driving down the highway and you are approaching a tollbooth. In a single-threaded "road," you have to wait your turn behind the five other drivers to pay the toll at the single tollbooth.
>
> In a multi-threaded "road," as you and the other drivers approach the toll both, five separate tollbooths suddenly open up to accommodate all the drivers simultaneously. If there were eleven drivers, eleven tollbooths would open up.

New Ways to Communicate

We are in the beginning stages of a new medium. The digital medium and the rules of communication are changing. What has not changed is our need to communicate—a need to share stories, to teach, and to learn.

I believe that these new and different ways will take advantage of one or more of the following seven unique attributes of new media:

- **Infinite space.** We are no longer constrained by newsprint space, or broadcast minutes, or magazine pages. The Web and emerging technologies are made to fit in our hand and deliver the world.

- **Interactivity.** Interactivity gives us the ability to respond to our audience. This covers everything from online discussions or chats to the ability to choose which pages to view and in which order. As a content developer, you can give users more control over their experience as information consumers.

- **Nonlinear communication.** Information does not need to be organized with a beginning, middle, and end—or solely organized the way one author thinks is appropriate. Different people's minds work in different ways; nonlinear presentations enable people to navigate through information in different ways.

- **Multimedia.** This is the first communication medium whose distribution channel is (at least potentially) independent of the type of content that is pumped through the channel. It is a powerful opportunity to choose the delivery that is most effective for getting across the points we want to make (be it text, graphics, audio, video, animation, or dynamic data).

- **The ability to present data.** This is the ability to analyze, understand, process, and present data. Searchable databases are among the most compelling products you can offer on the Web.

- **An immersive experience.** As storytellers, designers, developers, and creative minds, we deliver compelling information experiences. The same attributes that make video games addictive can be applied to educational or informative projects.

- **The ability to link content and commerce.** The Internet is the first medium that potentially allows the entire purchase cycle to be conducted in one setting—from awareness to trial to purchase, and even to post-purchase customer support. This offers an opportunity to link content directly to commerce and to generate revenue.

The promise of broadband is at hand. The tools to create new media continuously grow to be friendlier and more accessible. Yet, the power of this new medium remains mostly untapped. Every now and then the Web presents a glimpse at the promise of new media storytelling. Consider the "Books of Hope" (**www.britannica.com/hope**) as a shining example. What made this project work so well was the marriage of great content and an interactive design to navigate through and package. The fluid motion between scenes, the visual presentation of graphics and words, the use of typography, and the use of music and audio come together to build a Web experience that truly demands an emotional response from the audience. However, the essential element that holds the entire piece together is the content. This is not art for art's sake. So much of what we see on the Web is pure fluff and no content, a hodge-podge of bells and whistles. The "Books of Hope" is a forum for ideas and thoughts of 16 of the world's most respected thinkers (along with the Britannica.com audience). (See Figure 7.6.)

FIGURE 7.6   *The "Books of Hope" at Britannica.com was created using the offline Generator workflow process described in this book.*

Content, packaged and delivered through new media, that's the goal. This is what you do: design and develop. The objective is to clearly communicate the ideas and brand of your clients and projects through functional, scalable, and simple information design. This book steps you through development and design and presents a proven workflow methodology. The final ingredient comes from you and/or the client: content.

Chapter Summary

In this chapter, you explored the following topics:

- **Generator workflow.** This chapter reviewed the six steps in the workflow process. It also shared ideas, common practices, and tips involved in real-world design and development. Finally, this chapter discussed the integration of the workflow steps and their place in the process.

- **Building on your knowledge.** Using ideas and concepts from the workflow process, you should be able build tools for automated site development to produce projects with dynamic Flash movies, images, and content. Many of the same ideas learned here can be used for your work with online Generator as well.

- **Content is king.** Compelling sites and projects are not about bells and whistles. The excitement over cool effects never lasts for very long. In the end, it is all about content. The workflow process is about communicating, storytelling, learning, and teaching for the twenty-first century.

The workflow process for dynamic site development using Macromedia Generator and Flash described in this book is for the community of designers, developers, project managers, producers, and storytellers. This book was conceived with the sincere hope to share a wealth of knowledge and the tools to build interactive stories with content to those everywhere. Sadly, we have come to the end. This is just the beginning, however, for you and the next great Generator/Flash site. We wish you and your team all the best!

APPENDIX A

ActionScript for the Employee Navigation Main Screen

Navigation Duplication ActionScript

```
while (n < total) {
    n = (n)+1;
    bn = "dup" + n;
    duplicateMovieClip ("dup", bn, n);
    // space and position the duplicated clips
    setProperty (bn, _y, (getProperty(bn, _y))+n*(getProperty(bn,
_height)));
    set (bn add ":n", n);
}
// set up the scroll length variable
_root:dupH = _parent.roller.dup._height*total;
```

The Control Movieclip for Scrolling

```
startTop = _parent.scrollbg._y;
scrollWin = _parent.scrollbg._height;
if ((_parent.roller._y + _root:dupH) <= ((startTop + scrollWin) +
(_parent.roller.dup._y))) {
    gotoAndStop (1);
} else {
    setProperty (_parent.roller, _y, _parent.roller._y -20);
}

startTop = _parent.scrollbg._y;
if (_parent.roller._y <= startTop) {
    setProperty (_parent.roller, _y, _parent.roller._y +20);
} else {
    gotoAndStop (1);
}
```

The Button Actions

```
on (release) {
    loadMovieNum (eval("_parent.Link"+_name), 20);
}
on (rollOver) {
    this._xscale = this._xscale + 20;
    this._yscale = this._yscale + 20;
    overColor = new Color(this);
    overColor.setRGB(0x3399CC);
}
on (rollOut) {
    this._xscale = this._xscale - 20;
    this._yscale = this._yscale - 20;
    outColor = new Color(this);
    outColor.setRGB(0x999999);
}
```

APPENDIX B

Resources

Favorite Sites and Resources on the Web

Macromedia

Macromedia Exchange

http://www.macromedia.com/exchange/

The Exchange offers free extensions that enable you to add new features to Macromedia products.

Macromedia Generator

http://www.macromedia.com/software/generator

The site contains tech notes, a support center, white papers, and a discussion board.

Macromedia Generator Gallery

http://www.macromedia.com/software/generator/gallery/collection/

The Gallery contains case studies and links to a variety of Generator-developed Flash sites.

Development and Design Resources on the Web

Mike Chambers' Site

http://www.markme.com

Mike Chambers' site on Generator and Flash development. This site contains Generator tips of the day, including an AvantGo feed, several great Generator resources, and custom objects (such as an XML datasource).

FlashGen

http://www.flashgen.com

FlashGen is a site created in Flash with several good tutorials and examples.

Generator Developers Network

http://www.gendev.net

The Generator Developers Network contains plenty of Generator and Flash tutorials and examples.

Colon Moock's Site

http://www.moock.org

Colon Moock is a leader in interactive design and technology on the Web. His site is the source for incredible, in-depth how to information.

StarFish.com

http://www.starfish.com/

StarFish offers the Kimmuli tool—a visual tool for creating HTML, ASP, PHP, or ColdFusion dynamic datasources for Macromedia Generator and Flash.

The following Flash sites are all tremendous sources of tutorials, discussion boards, and incredible Flash design and technology:

ExtremeFlash

http://www.extremeflash.com/

FlashKit

http://www.flashkit.com/

FlashLite

http://www.flashlite.net

FlashMove

http://www.flashmove.com/gen/

FlashPlanet

http://www.flashplanet.com/

FlashZone

`http://www.flashzone.com`

Were-Here

`http://www.were-here.com/`

Dynamic Site Development Resources on the Web

Internet.com

`http://www.internet.com/sections/webdev.html`

A great launching pad to some of the best resource sites for dynamic technologies, reference materials, forums, and tutorials on the Web.

ScriptSearch

`http://scriptsearch.internet.com/`

This is a nice collection of server-side scripts.

SQL Course

`http://www.sqlcourse.com/`

This site gives you the skinny on SQL, including an introduction and tutorial.

WebDeveloper.com

`http://www.webdeveloper.com`

WebDeveloper.com is a nice resource site for Web developers. It provides industry news, technical articles, and a slew of information about everything Web-related.

WebMonkey's Guide to Web Programming

`http://hotwired.lycos.com/webmonkey/programming/index.html`

WebMonkey's Guide to Backend Databases

`http://hotwired.lycos.com/webmonkey/backend/databases/`

Other Favorites on the Web

Balthaser Studios

`http://www.balthaser.com`

Not to be confused with www.balthesar.com! This site is simply one of the most impressive Flash-based Web sites on the Internet. Turn up the volume when you visit this site!

The Books of Hope on Britannica.com

`http://www.britannica.com/hope/`

This is an example of a large content site created with the offline Generator workflow process.

Orange Design

`http://www.orangedesign.com`

Lynda Weinman's Site

`http://www.lynda.com`

Lynda's site is a great place for all things on or about developing for the Web and interactive.

Favorite Resources on the Bookshelf

Access 2000: The Complete Reference (Complete Reference Series) by Virginia Andersen. Osborne McGraw-Hill, 1999; ISBN: 0078825121

Adobe, Illustrator, 9.0 Classroom in a Book by Adobe Creative Team. Adobe Press, 2000; ISBN: 0201710153

Adobe, Photoshop, 6.0 Classroom in a Book by Adobe Creative Team. Adobe Press, 2000; ISBN: 0201710161

ASP in a Nutshell: A Desktop Quick Reference (Second Edition) by A. Keyton Weissinger. O'Reilly, & Associates, 2000; ISBN: 1565928431

We are huge fans of these books. They are great as quick reference sources when all you need to see is the code.

Being Digital by Nicholas Negroponte. Vintage Books, 1995; ISBN: 0679439196

Negroponte is the founder of MIT's Media Lab. He is also a regular writer for *Wired* magazine, where this collection of articles stem from.

The ColdFusion® 4.0 Web Application Construction Kit by Ben Forta, Nate Weiss (Contributor), and David E. Crawford (Contributor). Que, 1998; ISBN: 078971809X

This book covers the basics for creating ColdFusion applications. Now that Macromedia and Allaire have joined forces, ColdFusion might become a bigger part of your Generator-bag-o-tricks.

<Creative HTML Design> by Lynda Weinman and William Weinman. New Riders Publishing, 1998; ISBN: 1562057049

From the new media's best teacher, this book shows you the basics for building a great Web site.

Designing Web Usability: The Practice of Simplicity by Jakob Nielsen. New Riders Publishing, 1999; ISBN: 156205810X

Understanding the digital medium and our audience is the key to great new media projects. Professor Nielsen explains it all.

Flash® Web Design by Hillman Curtis. New Riders Publishing, 2000; ISBN: 0735708967

Hillman Curtis is a true artist whose canvas is the digital medium. His work as a Flash evangelist has inspired me to tell stories and build the tools for creating for the Web.

FreeHand® 9 Authorized by Tony Roame. Peachpit Press, 2000; ISBN: 0201700344

Journalist's Guide to the Internet, A: The Net as a Reporting Tool by Christopher Callahan. Allyn & Bacon, 1998; ISBN: 0205282156

Mediamorphosis: Understanding New Media (Journalism and Communication for a New Century) by Roger Fidler. Pine Forge Press, 1997; ISBN: 0803990863

Call me a geek, but this is definitely one of the best books I've ever read. Mediamorphosis is a comprehensive look at both the past and future of new media technology and communication. It gives you a complete understanding of the digital age and hope for our work as digital journalists.

Microsoft® Access 2000 Developer's Guide by Edward Jones. IDG Books Worldwide, 1999; ISBN: 0764533215

A complete source and reference for developing with Microsoft Access.

New Masters of Flash by Joshua Davis, Eric Jordan, et al. Friends of Ed, 2000; ISBN: 1903450039

This is a very cool, very impressive showcase of some of the top Flash designers and developers on the scene today.

New Media Technology: Cultural and Commercial Perspectives (Part of the Allyn & Bacon Series in Mass Communication) by John Pavlik. Allyn & Bacon, 1997; ISBN: 020527093X

If you're looking for a comprehensive description of the technology and its influence on human communication, this book has it.

The Road Ahead (Second Edition) by Bill Gates. Penguin USA, 1996; ISBN: 0140257276

Love him or hate him, Bill Gates has had a tremendous impact on the world we live in and how we communicate. No matter what opinion you have of the Microsoft perspective, this book says a good deal about where we have been and more importantly, where we are going in the digital future.

Running Microsoft® Internet Information Server by Leonid Braginski and Matthew Powell. Microsoft, Press, 1998; ISBN: 1572315857

This book includes instruction for setting up your IIS server and running your Web site with plenty of tutorials, examples, and illustrations.

Stop Stealing Sheep & Find Out How Type Works by Erik Spiekermann and E. M. Ginger. Adobe Press, 1993; ISBN: 0672485435

This book is a wonderful visual guide and historical reference of typography. These guys will show you how easy it is to communicate through text.

SQL in a Nutshell: A Desktop Quick Reference by Kevin E. Kline and Daniel Kline Ph.D. (Contributor). O'Reilly, & Associates, 2000; ISBN: 1565927443

Vbscript in a Nutshell: A Desktop Quick Reference by Ron Petrusha, Paul Lomax, and Matt Childs. O'Reilly, & Associates, 2000; ISBN: 1565927206

Software and Vendor Information

Adobe® Systems Incorporated

345 Park Avenue
San Jose, CA 95110-2704
Tel: (408) 536-6000
Fax: (408) 537-6000

http://www.adobe.com

Allaire

275 Grove Street
Newton, MA 02466
Tel: (617) 219-2000
Fax: (617) 219-2100

http://www.allaire.com/

Macromedia, Inc.

600 Townsend Street
San Francisco, CA 94103
Tel: (415) 252-2000
Fax: (415) 626-0554

http://www.macromedia.com/

Microsoft® Corporation

One Microsoft Way
Redmond, WA 98052-6399
Tel: (425) 882-8080

http://www.microsoft.com/

Persits Software

2111 Jefferson Davis Hwy, Suite 617S
Arlington, VA 22202
Tel: (800) 268-0689 or (703) 412-1015
Fax: (703) 412-1038

http://www.persits.com/

APPENDIX C

What's on the CD-ROM

The accompanying CD-ROM is packed with all sorts of exercise files and products to help you work with this book and with Macromedia Generator and Flash. The following sections contain detailed descriptions of the CD's contents.

For more information about the use of this CD, please review the ReadMe.txt file in the root directory. This file includes important disclaimer information as well as information about installation, system requirements, troubleshooting, and technical support.

System Requirements

This CD-ROM was configured for use on systems running Windows NT Workstation, Windows 95, Windows 98, Windows 2000, and Macintosh.

In order to work with the ASP (Active Server Pages) files used in the construction of the mock employee site, you will need to copy the contents of the [CD-drive]:\employee\ folder to your Microsoft Personal Web Server or Internet Information Server (IIS). Personal Web Server software and Internet Information Server both support Active Server Pages.

Personal Web Server is Web server software that enables you to host a single Web site from your own computer. It is available on your Windows 98 installation CD-ROM and includes support for Active Server Pages (ASP) technology.

If you are running Windows 95 or NT, you can download a copy of Personal Web Server directly from the Microsoft Web site at **http://www.microsoft.com/windows/ie/pws**. If you are running Windows 2000, then you can install Internet Information Server (IIS) 5.0 that includes support for Active Server Pages technology.

The path to the employee site on your system should be similar to c:\Inetpub\wwwroot\employee. To learn more about publishing Web sites on IIS please refer to the documentation that installs with Personal Web Server (PWS) and Internet Information Server (IIS).

Loading the CD Files

To load the files from the CD, insert the disc into your CD-ROM drive. If autoplay is enabled on your machine, the CD-ROM setup program starts automatically the first time you insert the disc. You may copy the files to your hard drive, or use them right off the disc.

Note: This CD-ROM uses long and mixed-case filenames, requiring the use of a protected mode CD-ROM driver.

Exercise Files

This CD contains all the files you'll need to complete the mock employee site in *Generator/Flash Web Development*. These files can be found in the root directory's Employee folder.

The CD contains the complete mock employee site development and finished deploy files. The contents of the Employee folder contains the following directories and files:

- Microsoft Access database for the mock employee site
- Enter/Modify ASP pages for "Employee Default," "Personal Biography," Professional Biography," "Skills and Samples," and "In Their Own Words" sections
- Update ASP pages for "Employee Default," "Personal Biography," Professional Biography," "Skills and Samples," and "In Their Own Words" sections
- Templates and source files for the mock employee site
- ASP data source pages for templates
- The deploy folder contains the finished Employee site

Breakdown of Source Files by Chapter

Chapter 2

Chapter 2 discusses planning and storyboarding for the mock employee site. You can refer to the template found in the directory [CD-drive]:\employee\flash source.

Chapter 3

Chapter 3 covered the construction of the mock employee site database and the data source text files for Generator processing. You can find the finished version of the Microsoft Access database used to build the mock employee site in the directory [CD-drive]:\employee\employee_db.mdb. The Microsoft Active Server Pages data source files used for Generator processing can be found in the directory [CD-drive]:\employee\generator\.

Chapter 4

In Chapter 4 you learned about building the templates for the employee mock site. Your can refer to the original Flash source files in the directory [CD-drive]:\employee\flash source\. The finished template used to process the employee movies can be found in the directory [CD-drive]:\employee\employee Template.swt.

Chapter 5

Chapter 5 discussed the construction of the employee data-entry tool. The home page for the employee mock site data-entry tool can be found in the directory [CD-drive]:\employee\default.asp. The source files for entering and modifying employee data can be found in the directory [CD-drive]:\employee\aspEnterModify\. The source files for updating employee data can be found in the directory [CD-drive]:\employee\aspUpdates\.

Chapter 6

Chapter 6 brought all the pieces together and showed you how to preview Generated employee movies and process the final versions. You can view the source file for previewing templates in the directory [CD-drive]:\employee\empDefaultPreview.asp. You can view the source file for processing templates in the directory [CD-drive]:\employee\generator\make.swf.

Chapter 7

In the final Chapter you constructed the mock employee site for deployment onto your server. This package is reflected in the directory [CD-drive]:\employee\deploy\. You can access the mock employee site by clicking on the file index.htm found in the directory [CD-drive]:\employee\deploy\index.htm.

Third-Party Programs

This CD also contains several third-party programs and demos from leading industry companies. These programs have been carefully selected to help you strengthen your professional skills with Macromedia Generator and Flash.

Please note that some of the programs included on this CD-ROM are shareware-"try-before-you-buy"-software. Please support these independent vendors by purchasing or registering any shareware software that you use for more than 30 days. Check with the documentation provided with the software on where and how to register the product.

Mac

- **Bare Bones Software, Inc BBEdit**. BBEdit is an HTML and text editing solution that provides a variety of Web authoring features for your Mac. Directory: [CD-drive]:MAC\BBEdit\BBEdit 6.0 Demo.smi

- **Microsoft Internet Explorer Browser**. Directory: [CD-drive]:MAC\MS-IE 5\Internet Explorer 5

- **Netscape Communicator Browser**. Directory: [CD-drive]:MAC\Netscape-Communicator

PC

- **Allaire ColdFusion Server trial**. Allaire ColdFusion is a visual Web application server that includes a database with programming and debugging tools. Directory: [CD-drive]:\PC\Allaire-CF Server\cfserver-451sp2-win-ent-eval-us\

- **Allaire HomeSite 4.5**. Allaire Homesite is an award-wining HTML editor and site development application integrated with many leading Web technologies such as ASP, JSP, CFML, and WML. Directory: [CD-drive]:\PC\Allaire-Homesite 4.5\HomeSite-452-win-eval-us.exe

- **ASPUpload**. Active Server Pages (ASP) component for file uploads (http:// www. aspupload.com/). Directory: [CD-drive]:\PC\ ASPUpload

- **ODBC-JDBC Assistant**. A tool created by Andrew Stopford designed to generate code for creating a JDBC-ODBC connection in a Generator datasource (http://freespace.virgin.net/andrew.stopford/odbctool.html). Directory: [CD-drive]:\PC\Generator ODBC Quick Tool\odbchelper.exe\

> **note**
>
> **Allaire and Macromedia.** At the printing of this book, Macromedia's acquisition of Allaire was not yet finalized. The references in this book and on the accompanying CD-ROM to Homesite and ColdFusion reflect this pending acquistion.

- **ASP Flash Turbine**. ASP Flash Turbine is a tool for creating dynamic content in Flash from Active Server Pages (ASP) without Generator (http://www.blue-pac.com/products/aspturbine/download/default.htm). Directory: [CD-drive]:\PC\ASP Flash Turbine\aspturbine50.exe

- **PHP Flash Turbine**. PHP Flash Turbine is a tool for creating dynamic content in Flash from PHP script pages without Generator (http://www.blue-pac.com/products/phpturbine/default.htm). Directory: [CD-drive]:\PC\ ASP PHP Turbine\phpturbine50.exe \

- **Microsoft Internet Explorer Browser**. Directory: [CD-drive]:\PC\MS-IE 5\ie5setup.exe

- **Netscape Communicator Browser**. Directory: [CD-drive]:\PC\Netscape-Communicator\cc32d476.exe

- **StarFish**. StarFish (originally known as Kimmuli) is a tool created for creating ASP, PHP, or ColdFusion files directly from your SWT file (http://freespace.virgin.net/andrew.stopford/starfish.html). Directory: [CD-drive]:\PC\StarFish 1.0\install.bat

- **SwordFish**. SwordFish (originally known as Bodhi) is a COM component for calling offline Generator (http://freespace.virgin.net/andrew.stopford/SwordFish.html). Directory: [CD-drive]:\PC\SwordFish\

Read This Before Opening the Software

By opening the CD package, you agree to be bound by the following agreement:

You may not copy or redistribute the entire CD-ROM as a whole. Copying and redistribution of individual software programs on the CD-ROM is governed by terms set by individual copyright holders.

The installer, code, images, actions, and brushes from the author(s) are copyrighted by the publisher and the authors.

This software is sold as-is, without warranty of any kind, either expressed or implied, including but not limited to the implied warranties of merchantability and fitness for a particular purpose. Neither the publisher nor its dealers or distributors assumes any liability for any alleged or actual damages arising from the use of this program. (Some states do not allow for the exclusion of implied warranties, so the exclusion may not apply to you.)

The Generator/Flash Web Development Web Site

The Web site that adds to the value of this book contains resources for anyone using Macromedia Generator and Flash 5 for site development. You can visit the Web site at **www.generatorflashbook.com**. It contains a great deal of supplementary information that will help you understand the development workflow process discussed throughout the book. You can even modify the dynamic site on the fly. In the download section, you can download the complete source files, including the database, Flash templates, and Active Server Pages (ASP) data-entry Web application. Be sure to bookmark the *Generator/Flash Web Development* Web site for the latest in Generator and Flash development. As the product updates are released, we'll keep the mock employee site project current. Here is a list of what you will find on the site:

- A working version of the employee Web site that you build over the course of this book
- A link to Amazon.com, in case you want to order extra copies to give as gifts
- A download page containing the complete Mock Employee Site Source files
- Information about the authors
- A discussion of who the audience of this book is
- A discussion of topics covered in this book
- A summary of this book's contents
- A feedback email link directly to the authors
- Links to the authors' Web sites
- An interactive Flash case study of Generator/Flash Offline Site Development

Index

A

abstraction, 51
Access, 53, 65
accessing data from databases, 75-79
ACTION attribute, 137
actions, form-submit action, 145-146
actions layers, 94-96
ActionScript, 85
  actions layers, 95
  duplicateMovieClip, 97-101
  loadMovie, 102-105
  TellTarget, 101
  with statement, 101-102
ActionScript.com, 85
Active Server Pages. *See* **ASPs**
adding additional layers on top of masks, 93
Adobe Illustrator, bugs when using, 34
animation, templates, 116
appearance of storyboards, 34
ASP pages, data-entry tool, 137
  enter/modify content pages. *See* enter/modify content pages
  Main Welcome page, 137-142
  update pages, 146-148
ASP Web applications and databases, 140-141
ASPExec, 165
ASPGenIntegration, 174
ASPs (Active Server Pages), 55-58, 134-135
  data-entry tools, 135
  Request, 144
  supporting HTML, 170-172

attributes
  ACTION, 137
  of media, 188-189
  METHOD, 137
audiences, brainstorming, 22

B

benefits
  of data-entry tool, 185
  of offline generator mode, 11-14
biography pages, identifying elements of data-entry tool, 132-134
"Books of Hope" (Britannica.com), 189
brainstorming, 21, 179-180
  audiences, 22
  elements for sites, 22-23
  flowing ideas together, 23
  goals, 21
  keeping ideas in scope, 24
  scope creep, 25
Britannica.com, 6, 189
budgets, 24
bugs, when using Illustrator, 34
building databases, 65-66
  sample employee database, 66-75

C

choreographing movement, storyboards, 39
  spacing elements, 40-41
  transitions, 41-43

clean data entry, 125
examples of, 125-127
ColdFusion, 54
comma-delimited lists, 50
command-line output options, 162
command-line processing, 162-163
commands
generate, 163
RS.update, 147
Set Environment, 151
communication, attributes of media, 188-189
comparing Generator 2 Developer Edition and Generator 2 Enterprise Edition, 188
content, 186
displaying enter/modify content pages, 144-145
previewing, 151-155
content-entry fields, 148
image input, 148-150
input choices, 150-151
text input, 148
control, 98
copying layers, 91
CreateObject( ), 166
creating
queries as SQL statements, 76
scrolling lists, 97-98
storyboards, 33-38
templates, 31-33
curly braces ({ }), variables, 113
customizing, 110

D

data
organizing, 61-63, 124-125
clean data entry, 125-127
content-entry fields. See content-entry fields
previewing content, 151-155
relationships, 63-65
retrieving from databases, 75-79

data sources, 49-51
abstraction, 51
comma-delimited lists, 50
Generator
databases. See databases
RAD tools, 53
server-side scripting, 55-58
XML, 59-60
hard-coded static values, 50
HTTP URLs, 51-52
Java classes, 52
JDBC/ODBC URL, 51
data-entry tools, 124-125, 136
ASP pages, 137
enter/modify content pages. See enter/modify content pages
Main Welcome page, 137-142
update pages, 146-148
ASPs, 135
benefits of, 185
Generator processing, 158
goals, 136
identifying elements of, 128
biography pages, 132-134
employee default pages, 128-130
main navigation pages, 128
Skills and Samples pages, 130-132
images, 159
workflow processes, 184-185
Database Manager window, 76
database queries, enter/modify content pages, 143-144
databases, 48-49
Access, 53, 65
accessing data, 75-79
and ASP Web applications, 140-141
building, 65-66
sample employee database, 66-75
finding one to fit your project, 52-53
Oracle, 53
RAD tools, 53
roles of, 182
SQL Server, 53
workflow processes, 181-183

deleting unnecessary items from templates, 122

deploying sites, timed updates, 174

depth of layers, templates, 89

Design View window, 77

designing templates, 82-83

designs, 39. *See also* site design

dimensions, setting, 82

displaying content, enter/modify content pages, 144-145

dup, 98

duplicateMovieClip
  templates, 97-101
  variables, 99

dynamic content, incorporating into templates, 115-118

dynamic design versus static design, 43-44

dynamic elements, 83-84

dynamic Generator objects, 113

dynamic site development, 4-6
  Generator, 7

dynamic text, incorporating in templates, 118-121

E

Edit in Place function, 85-86, 117

elements
  for sites, brainstorming, 22-23
  positioning with Info panel, 117
  spacing in time, choreographing movement, 40-41

employee databases, sample of, 66-75

employee default pages, identifying elements of data-entry tools, 128-130

enter/modify content pages
  ASP pages, 143
  database queries, 143-144
  displaying content, 144-145
  form-submit action, 145-146
  header navigation, 144

events, onClick event, 165

examples of data entry, 125-127

Execute method, 166

expanding on workflow processes, 186

eXtensible Markup Language (XML), 59-60

F

field names, 48

field types, 48

fields, 48

FileString, 171-172

final Generator production, preparing for, 155-156

final production
  goals, 158
  preparing for, 159-161

finding databases to fit your project, 52-53

Flash, 2
  ActionScript, 85
  Edit in Place function, 85-86
  optimizing
    images, 106
    sound, 107-109

Flash movies, generating, 158

FlashKit.com, 85

focusing brainstorming ideas, 24

folder names, personalizing, 110

Form element, 137

form-submit action, enter/modify content pages, 145-146

formats for images, choosing, 107

formatting variables and values for Generator, 50

frame rate, 41
  setting, 82

freeware, ASPExec, 165
functionality schematics, 32
functions
  Edit in Place, 85-86, 117
  WriteToFile, 171-172

G

Generate command, 163
generating Flash movies, 158
Generator, 2
  command-line output options, 162
  command-line processing, 162-163
  dynamic elements, 83-84
  Generator processing, data-entry tool, 158
  offline mode, 9-11, 161-162
    benefits of, 11-14
  online mode, 8-9, 161, 187-188
  optimizing images, 106
  processing templates, 161-162
  server-scripted publishing, 164-170
  templates, 49
  variables, 84
  workflow processes for site development,
    20-21
Generator 2 Developer Edition, 7, 187
  versus Generator 2 Enterprise Edition, 188
Generator 2 Enterprise Edition, 7, 187
  versus Generator 2 Developer Edition, 188

Generator data sources
  databases. *See* databases
  RAD tools, 53
  server-side scripting, 55-58
  XML, 59-60
Generator objects, 110-111
  JPG objects, 111-112
  properties, 112
  replacing with dynamic Generator
    objects, 113
  templates, 117
  tips for working with, 114
GET method, 137
goals
  brainstorming, 21
  for templates, 115
  of data-entry tools, 136
  of final production, 158
  of site design, 39

H

hard returns, HTML, 171
hard-coded static values, 50
hardware requirements, 4
header navigation, enter/modify
  content pages, 144
HTML
  FileString, 171
  supporting, 170-172
HTTP URLs, 51-52

I

ideas, flowing together, 23
identifying elements of data-entry tools, 128
    biography pages, 132-134
    employee default pages, 128-130
    main navigation pages, 128
    Skills and Samples pages, 130-132
if statements, content-entry fields (input choices), 151
image input, content-entry fields, 148-150
images
    choosing formats, 107
    data-entry tool, 159
    location of, 159
    optimizing, 105-106
    Photoshop images, JPEG compression, 105-106
    storing outside of database, 62
incorporating
    dynamic content into templates, 115-118
    dynamic text into templates, 118-121
infinite space, 188
Info panel, positioning elements, 117
information architecture, organizing data, 65
input choices, content-entry fields, 150-151
instance-naming conventions, templates, 96-97
instances, 96
integrating all pieces of workflow process, 185
interactivity, 188
Invisible button, 98

J-K

J2EE (Java 2 Enterprise Edition), 58
Java classes, 52
Java Server Pages (JSP), 58
JDBC/ODBC URL data source type, 51
JPEG compression, Photoshop images, 105-106
JPG objects, 111-112
    properties, 112-113
JSP (Java Server Pages), 58

keyframes, titles, 96

L

layers
    actions layers, 94-96
    copying and pasting, 91
    masks, 92-94
    storyboards, 91
    templates, 89-92
      setting up new layers, 91
libraries, organizing, 109-110, 121
load order, specifying, 89
loadMovie, templates, 102-105
    sizes, 102
location of images, 159
lockType, 147
long paragraphs, content-entry fields, 148

M

Macintosh versus PC with Flash, 81
Macromedia Freehand, 34
Macromedia Dreamweaver UltraDev, 54
Main Welcome page, ASPs, 137-142

masks
 adding additional layers on top of, 93
 layers, 92-94
media, attributes of, 188-189
METHOD attribute, 137
methods
 Execute method, 166
 GET, 137
 POST, 137
Microsoft Access, 53, 65
Microsoft ASP, 55-58
Microsoft SQL Server, 53
Microsoft Visual Interdev, 54
minimum hardware and software requirements, 4
movement, choreographing, 39
 spacing elements in time, 40-41
 transitions, 41-43
movies
 Flash movies, generating, 158
 size of, 88
MP3 export option, 108
multimedia, 189
multithreaded functions, 188

N

naming conventions, instances, 96-97
navigation pages, identifying elements of data-entry tool, 128
nonlinear communication, 189

O

objects
 Generator objects. *See* Generator objects
 JPG objects, properties, 112-113

offline Generator mode, 9-11, 161-162
 benefits of, 11-14
offline site development versus online site development, 8-11
OLE-DB interfaces, 140-141
onClick event, 165
online Generator mode, 8-9, 161, 187-188
online site development versus offline site development, 8-11
opening Scene panel, 87
optimizing
 images, 105-106
 sound, 105-109
options, -param, 167-168
Oracle, 53
ORDER BY clause, 76
organizing
 data, 61-63, 124-125
  clean data entry, 125-127
  content entry fields. See content entry fields
  previewing content, 151-155
  relationships, 63-65
 libraries, 109-110, 121
out-of area text, 92

P

paragraphs, content-entry fields, 148
-param option, 167-168
Params variable, 168
pasting layers, 91
PC versus Macintosh with Flash, 81
personalizing folder names, 110
photo files, 62
Photoshop images, JPEG compression, 105-106

PHP (PHP: Hypertext Preprocessor), 58
placeholders, 49
Generator objects. *See* Generator objects
planning
for final Generator production, 155-156
transitions, 42
positioning elements, Info panel, 117
POST method, 137
Praystation.com, 85
preparing
for final production, 159-161
for site development, 17-19
previewing content, 151-155
primary keys, 48
specifying, 49
processing templates
Generator, 161-162
with Generator
command-line processing, 162-163
server-scripted publishing, 164-170
properties
Generator objects, 112
JPG objects, 112-113
Properties panel, 107
Publish Settings panel, 89

Q-R

queries, creating as SQL statements, 76

RAD (Rapid Application Development) tools, 53-54
record set (RS), 139
records, 48
referential integrity, 65
relationships, organizing data, 63-65
replacing Generator objects with dynamic Generator objects, 113

Request, ASPs, 144
requirements, hardware and software requirements, 4
retrieving data from databases, 75-79
roles of databases, 182
rollers, 98
RS (record set), 139
RS.update command, 147

S

sample employee databases, building, 66-75
Scene panel, opening, 87
scenes, templates, 86-89, 116
switching scenes, 89
scope creep, 25
scrolling lists, 97-98
SELECT statements, 75-76
server-scripted publishing, Generator, 164-170
server-side scripting, 55-58
Set Environment command, 151
short phrases, content-entry fields, 148
single functions, 188
single words, content-entry fields, 148
site design
dynamic versus static design, 43-44
goals of, 39
site development
benefits of offline Generator mode, 11-14
dynamic site development, 4-6
Generator, 7
final list of sections, 25-26
offline Generator site development, 2
online versus offline, 8-9, 11
setting the stage for, 17-19
storyboards. *See* storyboards
workflow processes, 20-21
brainstorming. See brainstorming

sites, deploying, 174
size
  loadMovie actions, 102
  of movies, 88
Skills and Samples pages, identifying
  elements of data-entry tool, 130-132
software requirements, 4
sound, optimizing, 105-109
Sound Properties panel, 108
spacing elements in time,
  choreographing movement, 40-41
specifying primary keys, 49
SQL Server, 53
Statements, SELECT statements, 75-76
static design versus dynamic design,
  43-44
static elements, 83-84
storing images outside of database, 62
storyboards, 30-31, 45, 87, 180-181
  appearnce of, 34
  choreographing movement, 39
    spacing elements, 40-41
    transitions, 41-43
  creating, 33-38
    with templates, 31-33
  dynamic versus static design, 43-44
  layers, 91
  site design, goals of, 39
summary of workflow processes,
  178-179
supporting HTML, 170-172
switching scenes, templates, 89
system checks, testing, 173

T

table names, 48
tables, 48
Tcl (Tool Command Language), 58
TellTarget, 101
templates
  animation, 116
  deleting unnecessary items, 122
  designing, 82-83
  duplicateMovieClip, 97-101
  Generator objects, 117
  Generator templates, 49
  goals for creating, 115
  incorporating
    dynamic content, 115-118
    dynamic text, 118-121
  instance-naming conventions, 96-97
  layers, 89-92
    actions layers, 94-96
    masks, 92-94
    setting up new layers, 91
  libraries, organizing, 121
  loadMovie, 102-105
  processing with Generator 2, 161-162
    command-line processing, 162-163
    server-scripted publishing, 164-170
  scenes, 86-89, 116
    switching, 89
  static elements, 83
  storyboards, 31-33
  templates
    designing, 82-83
    workflow processes, 183-184
  with statement, 101-102
  workflow processes, 183-184

testing, 173
    system checks, 173
    visual checks, 174
text input, content-entry fields, 148
Text Options panel, 119
timed updates, 174
**tips for working with Generator
    objects, 114**
titles, keyframes, 96
Tool Command Language (Tcl), 58
tools
    data-entry tool. *See* data-entry tool
    RAD tools, 53

U

UltraDev, 54
update pages, ASP pages, 146-148
updates, timed updates, 174

V

values, formatting for Generator, 50
variables
    curly braces, 113
    duplicateMovieClip, 99
    formatting for Generator, 50
    Generator, 84
    Params, 168
vbcrlf (hard return), 171
visual checks, testing, 174
Visual Interdev, 54

W

Web sites. *See also* **site development**
    ActionScript.com, 85
    brainstorming elements for, 22-23
    FlashKit.com, 85
    Praystation.com, 85
WHERE filter clause, 76
white papers, ASPGenIntegration, 174
wholeroller, 98
**with statement, Flash templates,
    101-102**
workflow processes
    brainstorming, 179-180
    data-entry tool, 184-185
    databases, 181-183
    expanding on, 186
    integrating all pieces of process, 185
    site development, 20-21
        brainstorming. See brainstorming
    storyboards, 180-181
    summary of, 178-179
    template, 183-184
WriteToFile function, 171-172

X-Z

**XML (eXtensible Markup Language),
    59-60**

Intellistations.com

The Ultimate Internet Resource for Video, Film, 3D, and Creative Graphics Professionals

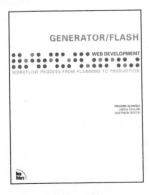

Buy Online via our secure ordering system for VISA, MC, and AMEX

Build your video/3D dream machine with our **Online Configurator**

Generator/Flash Web Development

Each New Riders book has been created with you, the computer graphics professional, in mind. Complete effects, adaptable solutions, time-saving techniques, and practical applications. Buy your favorite Generator/Flash book online today.

Generator/Flash Web Graphics Workstation

Build your own Web graphics workstation online and choose from a wide selection of the ultimate in processors, RAM, monitors, and graphics cards including Nvidia, Elsa, IBM, and 3DFX Voodoo.

Macromedia® Flash™ 5

Design and deliver distinctive, low-bandwidth Web sites with Macromedia Flash 5, the professional standard for producing high-impact Web experiences, used by over half a million Web authors. Top sites use Generator/Flash to produce engaging experiences that attract and excite Web users. An intuitive Macromedia user interface lets designers create engaging graphics easily, while server-side connectivity allows developers to create advanced Web applications.

Scanners, Tablets, and Printers

Check out IntelliStations.com for all of the latest tablets, printers, scanners, and enhancement plug-ins for Generator/Flash.

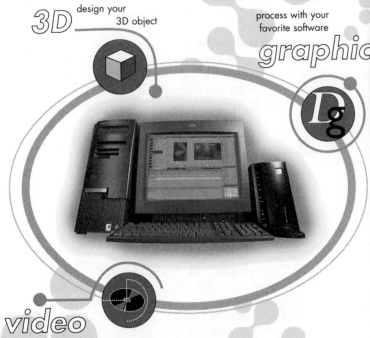

3D design your 3D object

process with your favorite software

graphic

video

output to DVD, CD-ROM, Web/Streaming media, or any other tape format

IntelliStations.com is your source for digital content creation tools that will allow your projects to be done on time, every time. The one you really want for video editing, 3D animation, Web design/graphics, and mo

Our knowledgeable technical production neers will also ASSIST you with INTEGRA of your IntelliStations.com system with you professional production equipment.

If you have questions while building your dream system, you can call us 24x7x365 1-800-501-0184 for assistance from one our IntelliStations.com DCC specialists. A about our no money down and creative financing programs.

Check out CGchannel.com, our content provider for 3D reviews, demos, and mo

 channel.com

 IBM Business Partner

 macromedia

 SONY Authorized Professional Reseller

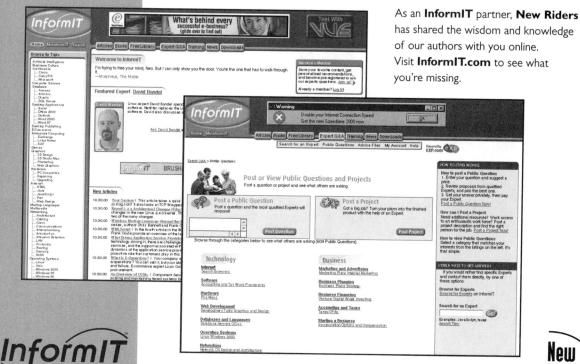

The **Voices**

that Matter

in a World of

Technology

Flash

Flash Web Design:
The v5 Remix
Hillman Curtis
0735710988, $45.00

Flash 5 Magic
Scott Hamlin and
David Emberton
0735710236, $45.00

Flash ActionScript
for Designers:
Drag, Slide, Fade
Brendan Dawes
0735710473, $45.00

Inside Flash 5
Fig Leaf Software
0735711054, $45.00

Flash to the Core
Josh Davis
0735711046, $45.00